OXFORD ENGLISH MONOGRAPHS

OXFORD ENGLISH MONOGRAPHS

ELIZABETHAN ACTING. By B. L. JOSEPH. 1951

ÞORGILS SAGA OK HAFLIÐA.
Edited by URSULA BROWN. 1952

SIR ORFEO. Edited by A. J. BLISS. 1954

THE PETERBOROUGH CHRONICLE 1070–1154
Edited by CECILY CLARK. 1958

THE OLD ENGLISH APOLLONIUS OF TYRE
Edited by PETER GOOLDEN. 1958

THE SONNETS OF WILLIAM ALABASTER
Edited by G. M. STORY and HELEN GARDNER. 1959

DEFOE
AND THE NATURE
OF MAN

BY

MAXIMILLIAN E. NOVAK

OXFORD UNIVERSITY PRESS

1963

Oxford University Press, Amen House, London E.C.4

GLASGOW   NEW YORK   TORONTO   MELBOURNE   WELLINGTON
BOMBAY   CALCUTTA   MADRAS   KARACHI   LAHORE   DACCA
CAPE TOWN   SALISBURY   NAIROBI   IBADAN   ACCRA
KUALA LUMPUR   HONG KONG

PRINTED IN GREAT BRITAIN
AT THE UNIVERSITY PRESS, OXFORD
BY VIVIAN RIDLER
PRINTER TO THE UNIVERSITY

PREFACE

'I am most entertained with those Actions which give
me a Light into the Nature of Man.'
Daniel Defoe, *A Collection of Miscellany Letters,
Selected out of Mist's Weekly Journal*[1]

THE following study grew out of a search after the sources
for the ideas which appear in Defoe's fiction. Noting references
to Hugo Grotius and Samuel Pufendorf in Defoe's long poem,
Jure Divino, I decided to see if these writers might account for
some of his unusual theories of law and human behaviour.
Much to my surprise, I discovered what I feel to be the ideo-
logical basis for some of his best themes and stories.

While relying heavily on the philosophers of natural law, I
have tried, through a careful examination of Defoe's reading,
to trace every relevant source. Whenever possible I have supported my arguments from authors whom Defoe had mentioned
or quoted.

Since there is neither a complete edition nor a wholly satisfactory bibliography of Defoe's writings, I have had to use a
combination of modern editions and original sources. For
Defoe's fiction I have relied on the Shakespeare Head Edition
whenever possible, and for a bibliography, the *Cambridge
Bibliography of English Literature*, supplemented by the cata-
logues of the Bodleian, Boston Public, British Museum, William
Andrews Clark and Henry E. Huntington Libraries, and by
Professor John Robert Moore's helpful suggestions and his in-
valuable *Checklist of the Writings of Daniel Defoe*.

I am deeply indebted to the librarians of these institutions
and to Professor Moore. I also wish to thank the late Professor
Edward Niles Hooker and Professor H. T. Swedenberg, who
first interested me in Defoe, Mr. F. W. Bateson, who criticized
my earliest ideas on this subject, the Fulbright Commission,
whose grant enabled me to study in England, and the editors

[1] (1722–7), iii. 198.

of *Modern Philology*, *Philological Quarterly*, and *Studies in English Literature*, who have kindly permitted me to reprint sections of this work which have appeared in their journals. I owe my deepest debt of gratitude, however, to Professor Herbert Davis, whose helpful suggestions and encouragement have made this work possible.

                                                M. E. N.

PREFACE

'I am most entertained with those Actions which give
me a Light into the Nature of Man.'
Daniel Defoe, *A Collection of Miscellany Letters,
Selected out of Mist's Weekly Journal*[1]

THE following study grew out of a search after the sources
for the ideas which appear in Defoe's fiction. Noting references
to Hugo Grotius and Samuel Pufendorf in Defoe's long poem,
Jure Divino, I decided to see if these writers might account for
some of his unusual theories of law and human behaviour.
Much to my surprise, I discovered what I feel to be the ideo-
logical basis for some of his best themes and stories.

While relying heavily on the philosophers of natural law, I
have tried, through a careful examination of Defoe's reading,
to trace every relevant source. Whenever possible I have supported my arguments from authors whom Defoe had mentioned
or quoted.

Since there is neither a complete edition nor a wholly satisfactory bibliography of Defoe's writings, I have had to use a
combination of modern editions and original sources. For
Defoe's fiction I have relied on the Shakespeare Head Edition
whenever possible, and for a bibliography, the *Cambridge
Bibliography of English Literature*, supplemented by the cata-
logues of the Bodleian, Boston Public, British Museum, William
Andrews Clark and Henry E. Huntington Libraries, and by
Professor John Robert Moore's helpful suggestions and his in-
valuable *Checklist of the Writings of Daniel Defoe*.

I am deeply indebted to the librarians of these institutions
and to Professor Moore. I also wish to thank the late Professor
Edward Niles Hooker and Professor H. T. Swedenberg, who
first interested me in Defoe, Mr. F. W. Bateson, who criticized
my earliest ideas on this subject, the Fulbright Commission,
whose grant enabled me to study in England, and the editors

[1] (1722–7), iii. 198.

of *Modern Philology*, *Philological Quarterly*, and *Studies in English Literature*, who have kindly permitted me to reprint sections of this work which have appeared in their journals. I owe my deepest debt of gratitude, however, to Professor Herbert Davis, whose helpful suggestions and encouragement have made this work possible.

M. E. N.

CONTENTS

ABBREVIATIONS

Dent ed.   *Romances and Narratives by Daniel Defoe*. ed. George
                Aitken. 1895.

HLQ   *Huntington Library Quarterly*

JEGP   *Journal of English and Germanic Philology*

Lee   William Lee, *Daniel Defoe: His Life and Recently Dis-
                covered Writings*. 3 vols. 1869.

PMLA   *Publications of the Modern Language Association of
                America*

RES   *Review of English Studies*

Shakespeare
Head ed.   *The Shakespeare Head Edition of the Novels and
                Selected Writings of Daniel Defoe*. 14 vols. 1927.

SP   *Studies in Philology*

Tegg ed.   *The Novels and Miscellaneous Works of Daniel Defoe*.
                20 vols. 1841.

I

DEFOE AND THE LAWS OF NATURE

I

Law is the Result of Reason, and . . . the Sovereignty of
Reason over all the Actions of Men, cannot be invaded,
but that Laws offer'd by whatever Society of Men
against Reason, are void of course. . . .

DANIEL DEFOE, *Party Tyranny*[1]

ALTHOUGH Daniel Defoe was born in 1660, the year which
witnessed the collapse of the Puritan experiment in English
government and the restoration of the Stuarts to the throne,
he is frequently discussed as if he were the intellectual contemporary of Bunyan and Milton. The result has been a strange
inability to associate Defoe the moralist with Defoe the novelist.
Examined for their Puritan morality, his novels and their
author have been judged lacking in sensitivity and discrimina-
tion. Recently, Mr. Louis Kronenberger has ventured the suggestion that Defoe's novels contain little Puritan morality or,
for that matter, morality of any kind.[2] On the other hand, critics
and biographers who have approached Defoe's novels through
his religious ideas have sometimes failed to comprehend how he
could have written fiction at all. The problem suggested by
these contradictions is whether there is any standard of morality
in Defoe's fiction, and if there is, what relationship exists between his morality and his theology.

I believe that the answer to this central problem may be
found in Defoe's use of natural law. Throughout his writings
on politics, economics, and practical morality there is an appeal
to the laws of nature, sometimes called the laws of reason. *Jure*

---

[1] In *Narratives of Early Carolina*, ed. Alexander Salley (1911), p. 229.
[2] *Kings and Desperate Men* (1959), p. 144.

Divino, his longest and most ambitious work on political theory, begins with a dedication to reason, 'Image of, and Ambassador Extraordinary from, the Maker of all Things: The Almighty's Representative and Resident in the Souls of Men, and one of Queen NATURE's most Honourable Privy Council.'[1] Reason, he says, is the one monarch ruling by divine right, and any laws which contradict the laws of reason '*are* ipso facto *void in their own Nature*'.[2] More often than not these statements concerned a specific body of legal thought known as natural law. During the seventeenth century, writers like Grotius, Cumberland, and Pufendorf elevated natural law into a complete code of behaviour, a code based on a universal reason with its origins in human nature and God. Whatever laws of society or even Christianity opposed the law of nature could not require either man's obedience or respect. Thus natural law acted as a catalyst in the revolutions and legal reforms of the next two centuries.[3]

As a child of his age, Defoe formulated his own scheme of natural law, and by borrowing, combining, and emphasizing various concepts in the writings of Grotius, Hobbes, Locke, and many other philosophers, he was able to achieve a certain eclectic originality. My purpose in the following study is to suggest that the answer to the problem of morality in Defoe's fiction may be found in his allegiance to the laws of nature; it is by this standard that almost all of Defoe's characters must be judged. Although this problem is complicated by the religious beliefs of the narrators, which results in a confusion between two valid but separate moral systems, once we understand what Defoe meant by natural law and natural morality, we can evaluate the morality of a given action far better than the

---

[1] Daniel Defoe, Dedication, *Jure Divino* (1706), p. [1].
[2] Ibid., p. [2].
[3] For general discussions of the development of theories of natural law during this period see Otto Gierke, *Natural Law and the Theory of Society, 1500–1800* (1950); and Leo Strauss, *Natural Right and History* (1953). For the Middle Ages see Robert Carlyle and A. J. Carlyle, *A History of Medieval Political Theory in the West* (1950), i. 8–169; ii. 28–137; v. 5–27, 440.

narrators themselves. In this first chapter, therefore, I intend to establish Defoe's general opinions on natural law and human nature as they appear in his didactic works and, in the following chapters, proceed to a detailed examination of his fiction, showing how these ideas manifested themselves in the world of Robinson Crusoe and Moll Flanders, Colonel Jack and Roxana.

II

Christians deviate from thy Rules, and dishonour even that Nature, whose Dictates they know as well as feel in their own Breasts equally with other Creatures!

DEFOE, *The Conduct of Christians Made the Sport of Infidels*[1]

IN medieval Christian thought the law of nature was regarded as a law of reason written in the hearts of men by God. Richard Hooker, who summarizes the medieval concept of natural law, argued that it was more correctly called 'the Law of Reason', since it included 'all those things which men by the light of their natural understanding evidently know'.[2] Scholastic philosophy rejected the idea that natural law applied only to those laws which man had in common with animals as well as the views of the strict conventionalists who maintained that all law was merely the custom of an individual nation. The result was a reliance on a standard which was universal and superior to the *jus gentium*, the positive laws of different countries.

This concept of a universal standard of reason had strong attractions for the Puritans. A glance at William Ames's *Conscience*, a Puritan classic, will show how well natural law suited the Calvinistic view of man.[3] Ames defined the law of nature as 'that Law of God, which is naturally written in the hearts of all men'.[4] But he distinguished between an '*Inlightened*' and a

---

[1] (1717), p. 8.

[2] *Laws of Ecclesiastical Polity* (1954), i. 182 (I. viii. 9).

[3] For a discussion of Ames's wide influence see Arthur Barker, *Milton and the Puritan Dilemma* (1942), pp. 28, 306–7.

[4] (1643), I. ii. 4.

'*Naturall*' conscience. The enlightened conscience has, in addition to the knowledge of nature, the supports of the gospel and faith, while the natural conscience has to rely merely on an inner knowledge of right to struggle against the passions. In spite of the laws of nature being 'ingraffed and imprinted in the Nature of man, by the God of Nature', it was usually assumed that the guidance of natural principles was insufficient to overrule the passions. And when man was so ruled by his passions that he committed sins which even the beasts avoided, his sins were 'exceedingly aggravated'.[1] Thus while Ames rejected the idea that the laws of nature merely concerned those elements which man had in common with animals, he retained this older concept of natural law as a useful standard.

Ames believed that these laws were clear and certain, discoverable by the use of right reason even among 'the more understanding sort of the Heathen'. But although the laws are obvious, man's heart has been corrupted by Adam's Fall. Hence it was necessary to record the laws of nature, as was done in the laws of Moses:

> That to Nature upright, (*i.e.*) *as it was in the State of innocency*, there was no need of such a Promulgation. But ever since the corruption of our Nature, such is the blindnesse of our understanding and perversnesse of our will and disorder of our affections, that there are onely some Reliques of that Law remaining in our hearts like to some dimme aged picture....[2]

This image of the Fall and the dim 'Reliques' of the laws of nature led to a division between the primary and secondary laws of nature, the first for man as he would have been had he remained in the Garden of Eden, the second for the corrupted nature of man. It was invariably in this sense of a law for a corrupt mankind, separated from grace, that Puritans accepted natural law.

This view of natural law had been rejected by many earlier writers. Cornelius Agrippa listed the maxims of 'the corrupt

---

[1] (1643), v. i. 16.
[2] Ibid., v. i. 28.

Law of Nature', arguing that it was merely a law of enlightened self-interest:

Keep off force by force. Break faith with him that breaks faith. To deceive the deceiver is no deceit. A deceiver is not bound to a deceiver in ought. A fault may be recompensed by a fault. Those that deserve ill ought to enjoy neither justice nor faith. No injury can be done to the willing. He that buys may deceive himself. A thing is worth so much as it may be sold for. A man may provide for his safety with the damage of another. No man is oblig'd to impossibilities. Thou or I are to be ruined, it is better that thou be ruin'd than I.[1]

Such a theory, Agrippa contended, would overthrow all religion, establishing in its place an *'Epicurean* Pleasure for supreme Happiness'.[2] But Agrippa's insistence that all human laws were conventional was unsatisfactory to an age which was seeking a scientific solution to problems of ethics and laws.

Throughout the seventeenth century natural law became the standard for man's life as a political and social animal. Whereas Grotius, writing at the beginning of the century, still emphasized duties and obligations imposed on man by the law of nature, Hobbes and Locke also spoke of rights, or freedom from obligation. Thus natural law evolved into an explosive political and moral doctrine, insisting on the individual's rights of self-defence and self-preservation. Grotius rejected self-interest as the basis for natural law as did later writers like Cumberland and Shaftesbury, who suggested benevolence as a primary principle. But the theories of self-interest and self-defence suited so well with the Calvinistic concept of man in his fallen state under the secondary laws of nature that it is not surprising to find Defoe among those who constructed their systems of politics and ethics on a foundation of *amour de soi*.

The religious basis of the laws of nature was always acknowledged but frequently ignored. In *Jure Divino* Defoe asks why the tyrant is not destroyed by God. His answer reveals an attitude which Defoe maintained throughout his life; it may be

---

[1] Henry Cornelius Agrippa, *The Vanity of Arts and Sciences* (1676), p. 317.
[2] Ibid., p. 318.

summed up in the proverb, 'God helps those that help themselves':

> Prayers and Tears no Revolutions make,
> Pull down no Tyrants, will no Bondage Break;
> Heaven never will our faint Petitions hear,
> Till Just Endeavours supersede our Prayer;
>
> .   .   .   .   .
>
> Christians must no more Miracles expect,
> And they that will be Slaves, he'll not protect;
> They that would have his Power to be their Friend,
> Must with what Power they have their Right Defend;
> In vain they for Divine Assistance stay,
> Unless they learn to fight as well as pray.[1]

The world in which Defoe's characters move is one which operates almost exclusively by second causes. 'God', wrote Defoe, 'has subjected even the ways of his Providence to Rational Methods, and Outward Means agree to it. The great Chain of Causes and Effects, is not interrupted, even by God himself; if it be, it is on Extraordinary Occasions, which we call Miracles.'[2] Whatever happens in the world is ultimately the act of God. Defoe reminded the reader that '. . . nothing can happen to you but what comes from Providence, and consists with the interest of the universe',[3] and elsewhere, that '. . . life and all the contingencies of life are subjected to the dominion of Providence. . . '.[4] But Defoe's Providence works entirely through nature and is often indistinguishable from nature. Although he drew a firm distinction between his own theory of God as 'Nature Naturing' and the pantheist's 'Nature Natured', Defoe's decision to seek God in natural causes results in almost the same view of the phenomenal world.[5]

Nevertheless, the God of Defoe's nature is always present in

---

[1] Bk. ii, p. 19.
[2] Defoe, The Danger of the Protestant Religion, in A True Collection of the Writings of the Author of the True Born English-man (1703–5), i. 254.
[3] Defoe, The Dumb Philosopher, in Romances and Narratives by Daniel Defoe, ed. George Aitken (1895), xv. 210. Subsequent references to this edition of Defoe's writings will be cited as Dent ed.
[4] The Compleat English Tradesman, 2nd ed. (1727), i. 232.
[5] Defoe, A Review of the Affairs of France, ed. Arthur Secord (1938), iii. 5b.

his works. Calvin had contended that 'Fortune and Chance are heathen terms. . . . For if all success is blessing from God, and calamity and adversity are his curse, there is no place left in human affairs for Fortune and Chance.'[1] If any of Defoe's fictional characters fall into difficulties, Defoe will present a variety of natural causes to explain the situation, but the final cause is God. For example, when Captain Gow, the pirate, is captured, Defoe muses on God's role in the world: '. . . Heaven having by a visible infatuation upon themselves, and a concurrence of other circumstances, brought them all into the hands of justice.'[2] Success is the test of all action for Defoe, for it reveals God's will. Even such a trivial matter as Moll Flanders's 'luck' in gambling is ultimately reducible to her favour with God.

Defoe's 'nature' is a hodge-podge of traditional Puritanism, the rationalism of the Boyle Lectures, and the ideas of Thomas Burnet. Although he had some reservations about Burnet's *Sacred Theory of the Earth*, Defoe was inevitably attracted to a theory of the Deluge which successfully mingled science and theology and which showed how God worked through second causes. Burnet's scheme proclaimed a Golden Age which existed until the Deluge, with the antediluvians residing on an earth without large mountains or seas in a climate of perpetual spring, or what Defoe called 'a Paradise in its Degree'.[3] He accepted Burnet's argument on the ruin and destruction of the earth after the Deluge in his moral works, while maintaining throughout his economic writings that the earth was the best of all possible worlds in relation to commerce. In addition to attacking Burnet on the idea that the irregularity of coasts and harbours was an indication of the cracked frame of the world, Defoe contended that '. . . the wise Creator has most evidently shewn to us, that he design'd the World for Commerce'.[4] Like

[1] John Calvin, *Institutes of the Christian Religion*, trans. Henry Beveridge (1953), i. 179.

[2] *Adventures of Captain John Gow*, Dent ed., xvi. 335.

[3] William Lee, *Daniel Defoe: His Life, and Recently Discovered Writings* (1869), iii. 133. Cf. Thomas Burnet, *The Sacred Theory of the Earth*, 3rd ed. (1697), pp. 121–5.

[4] *A General History of Trade*, No. 1 ([August?] 1713), p. 10.

the contemporary theologian, John Clarke, Defoe seems to have believed that the image of a curse on the earth after the Fall was only 'comparatively spoken'.[1]

It might be expected from Defoe's sermons on the 'Divinity of Trade' that he would have accepted the latitudinarian argument in regard to the plurality of worlds. Burnet had referred to earth as 'our dirty little Planet', criticizing the pride of man who could think that the earth was the only 'habitable part of the Universe', while John Clarke and Locke agreed that it was a 'reasonable Conjecture' that beings of a superior order existed on other planets.[2] But Defoe attacked this idea in Robinson Crusoe's 'Vision of the Angelic World' and several other works as a complete absurdity:

> I may as well ask the Enquirer what sort of Inhabitants they are who possess the Moon or any of the Planets, and whether they dwell in a State of Innocence, or have contracted Guilt; and if the latter, whether there is a glorious Establishment of Redemption, and a Covenant of Life granted for them, as there is here, by the Purchase and Merit of a Saviour?[3]

Defoe concludes that it is more probable that God would have created a waste than that he would have made a new species for each planet.

In attacking current speculations on the plurality of worlds, Defoe set himself against the theory of cosmic plenitude, the great theme of the Boyle Lectures. He kept abreast of all the new ideas of his day, but retained his faith in his conscience and the Bible. And while he defended the Bible against the attacks of the deists, he apparently felt free to use concepts like primitivism, a voyage to the moon, or even deism for special effects.

---

[1] Clarke, *An Enquiry into the Cause and Origin of Moral Evil* (1720–1), i. 207.

[2] Burnet, *Sacred Theory*, p. 104. See also Clarke, *Enquiry into Moral Evil*, i. 104.

[3] *An Essay on the History and Reality of Apparitions*, 2nd ed. (1729), p. 53.

III

> It is very plain, that the effect of that first man's sin is a
> corrupt taint, which we all bring into the world with us,
> and which we find upon our nature, by which we find
> a natural propensity in us to do evil, and no natural in-
> clination to do good. . . .
>
> DEFOE, *The Family Instructor*[1]

ALTHOUGH Defoe never wrote a religious epic on the Creation
and Fall of man in the manner of *Paradise Lost*, scattered
throughout his numerous writings are enough references to
this theme to construct a thorough system. The Devil was able
to tempt man because he was able to perceive the dualism of
human nature,

. . . how mixt up of a Nature convertible and pervertible, capable
indeed of infinite Excellence, and consequently of eternal Felicity;
but subject likewise to Corruption and Degeneracy, and consequently to eternal Misery.[2]

As in Milton's scheme, Adam and Eve as well as the antediluvians perceived knowledge directly. After the Flood, however,

In the room of this capacious Understanding and this inquiring
and applying Temper in those Ages, behold a stupid Generation
risen up in Succession; stript as naked of the natural Glories of
their Ancestors, as the Earth was of its natural Fruitfulness after the
Curse in *Paradise*; and instead of applying themselves to useful
Arts, and to the acquiring of Knowledge, grown as indolent as they
were ignorant, having, like *Solomon's* Fool, no delight in Understanding.[3]

Deprived of this intuitive knowledge, men tried to replace it
with reason. But in this religious scheme, except for occasional
glimmerings of reason, man is a fool. Thus reason, man's
highest faculty, is entirely insufficient for judging matters of
religion. The idea of the wise pagan interested Defoe, but he

---

[1] *The Novels and Miscellaneous Works of Daniel Defoe* (1841), xv. 21.
Subsequent references to this edition of Defoe's writings will be cited as
Tegg ed.

[2] *The Political History of the Devil* (1726), p. 99.

[3] *A System of Magick* (1727), p. 11.

used Numa Pompilius as a paradigm of the man who may ascend the heights of reason while remaining a fool in his religion. 'When Men Pore upon the Sacred Mysteries of Religion with the Mathematical Engines of Reason', Defoe remarked, 'they make such incoherent stuff of it, as would make one pity them.'[1]

Defoe was never able to conclude with Pope and the Boyle Lecturers that the existence of evil in the universe was to be explained by 'universal good'. He mocked at Milton's attempts to explain how evil entered the universe, suggesting that it must have preceded the creation of the world:

> Tell us, sly penetrating Crime,
> How cam'st thou there, thou fault sublime?
> How didst thou pass the Adamantine Gate,
> And into Spirit thy self insinuate?
>
> .   .   .   .   .   .
>
> Sure there was once a time when thou wert not,
> By whom wast thou created? and for what?
> Art thou a steam from some contagious damp exhal'd?
> How should contagion be intail'd,
> On bright seraphic Spirits, and in a place
> Where all's supreme, and Glory fills the Space?[2]

Although he apparently never succeeded in solving to his satisfaction the problem of cosmic evil, he was fully content with the traditional Puritan idea of original sin as an explanation of human depravity. '*The Imagination of the Heart of Man is Evil*', he quoted, '*and only Evil, and that continually.*'[3]

Defoe's theory that the human race was 'one corrupted Mass' was good Calvinistic theology, but it was in distinct opposition to the thought of his time. By 1719, when *Robinson Crusoe* first appeared, most writers acquiesced in Richard Cumberland's theory that man was governed by a regard for the common good of society as well as a '*limited Self-Love*', and Shaftesbury's and

---

[1] *An Enquiry into the Case of Mr. Asgil's General Translation* (1704), p. 8.
[2] *Political History of the Devil*, p. 66. See also Defoe's journal *The Commentator*, No. 40 (20 May 1720).
[3] *Jure Divino*, bk. vii, p. 4. See Genesis vi. 5.

Hutcheson's doctrine of the 'moral sense' was soon to become the prevailing mode of thought.[1] To the school of sentimentalists, man was naturally good, and benevolence was the primary human characteristic. Defoe, on the contrary, rejected the idea of the 'good natured' man. In a passage from the *Review*, he pretended not to understand what the term could mean: 'as in its literal Sense, it is Nonsense and Contradiction; Nature being in its Constitution corrupt'.[2] He stated his position most clearly in an attack on Shaftesbury's idea that man's natural goodness is corrupted by civilization:

The learned may talk of the rectitude of Nature and of natural religion in bar of the principle which others insist upon, that nature is originally deprav'd: I am for putting it to the generall issue, if they can tell me by any one example when nature of its meer undirected inclination guided mankind to make the best choice of things, and rejecting the pleasing objects of sence led him to choose vertue by a meer propensity of will without instruccion or example; then I may come into the notion of natural rectitude with some appearance of reason.[3]

Defoe insists that until he is shown evidence to the contrary he will continue to believe that there is '. . . something of originall depravity in nature more than those gentlemen think of'.[4] Corruption, not virtue, is natural to man.

Betrayed by his passions, man learns that without the aid of religion reason is not strong enough to guide him to virtue. Even the religious man remains corrupt and erring, for, as Defoe confessed, 'Religion has not so much chang'd our Natures'.[5] Charles Morton, Defoe's teacher, wrote a treatise on the passions in which he showed how sanctification could transform the passions into virtues. Defoe seldom made this arbitrary division between the passions before and after sanctification.

---

[1] Richard Cumberland, *A Treatise of the Laws of Nature*, trans. John Maxwell (1728), p. 335 (viii. 7). See also Ernest Tuveson, 'The Origins of the Moral Sense', *HLQ*, xi (May 1948), 242–59.

[2] 'Little Review', ii. 21*b*.

[3] *The Compleat English Gentleman*, ed. Karl Bülbring (1890), p. 111.

[4] Ibid., p. 112.

[5] *Some Considerations upon Street-Walkers* (1726), p. 15.

Nor did he believe that an act of passion was in any way ex-
cusable. Every man is responsible for his acts,

> . . . for else all the wickedness we can commit in the world may have
> the unnatural temper and constitution of the man to plead in its
> excuse. The murderer will excuse himself by his being of a passionate
> temper. . . . The drunkard will plead the heat of his constitution;
> the thief, an avaricious temper; the debauched rake, the acrimony
> of his blood, and the like. Nature is vitiated and tainted with variety
> of infirmities; whether originally, and by descent from the first
> man, is not our present subject, but so it is; there are powerful
> inclinations to do evil in every one, and where these are not governed
> by the power of our reason or sense of religion, they become our
> governors and push us upon unavoidable folly; so far these natural
> inclinations are sinful, and we must oppose, restrain, watch against,
> and struggle with them, and the omission of that opposition is a
> great sin.[1]

The use of the reason in combating the passions is a categorical
imperative, and those who deny this command fit into the
category which Defoe reserved for 'Fools'.

These 'Fools' are people who are ruled by their passions or
their love of pleasure. Because of man's depravity, this category
includes almost the entire human race:

> But since Mankind are all alike so frail,
> That Crimes with Life come like Estates in tail;
> All have an equal Title to Reproach,
> Except some few, who sin a Knot too much:
> He that has all his own Mistakes confest,
> Stands next to him who never has transgresst,
> And will be censur'd for a Fool by none,
> But they who see no Errors of their own:
> For Innocence in Men cannot be meant
> Of such as ne're offend, but as repent.[2]

Repentance, then, is the answer to man's frailty and along with
faith, the necessary article in Defoe's concept of Christianity.
Unlike many religious thinkers of his time, he believed that

---

[1] *Family Instructor*, Tegg ed., xvi. 190.
[2] *More Reformation*, in *A True Collection*, ii. 36.

since repentance was a spiritual gift of God which need be made only once, the death-bed repentance would be accepted by God as a true act of remorse. 'He will receive us, however late, and by whatever necessity or distress we are driven', says one of his characters, and although Defoe admitted that the death-bed was not the best place for contrition, he was willing to accept any kind of genuine repentance.[1]

This emphasis on repentance contains an inherent opposition to the theory of the 'good natured' man. For Defoe virtue without religion was 'negative' virtue. Crusoe attacks those virtuous men who believe that they are fundamentally different from the highwayman.[2] All men sin, Crusoe argues, and it is better to fall into sin, realize it, and repent than to believe that one has never sinned at all.

> Thieves, Highway-men, and Murtherers are sent
> To *Newgate* for their future Punishment,
> But all Men pity them when they repent.[3]

Thus in his lives of Shepperd, Wild, and Gow, three famous criminals of the time, Defoe was careful to report the repentance of Shepperd and to arouse the pity of the reader for him, while condemning Wild and Gow as vicious and beyond redemption.

In his attitude towards original sin and repentance, Defoe was clearly a writer in the Puritan tradition, but his Puritanism was that of a contemporary of Locke and Thomas Burnet. He was enormously influenced by the rationalism of his day. Although he argued that the Bible was infallible, he questioned whether the story of Babel was an adequate explanation for the variety of languages, laughed at Bunyan's cloven-footed Devil, attacked the idea that Heaven was a place inhabited by angels playing harps, and refused to commit himself to a rigid doctrine of predestination. His remarks on the treatment of witches are in the best spirit of rationalism.[4]

[1] *Due Preparations for the Plague*, Dent ed., xv. 133.
[2] *Serious Reflections of Robinson Crusoe*, Dent ed., iii. 163.
[3] *More Reformation*, in *A True Collection*, ii. 63.
[4] Although he believed in the existence of witches, he regarded the trial

IV

The Laws of God, as I can understand,
Do never Laws of Nature countermand;
Nature Commands, and 'tis Prescrib'd to Sense,
For all Men to adhere to *Self-defence*.

DEFOE, Jure Divino¹

AT the beginning of a brief discussion of the origin of government in the *Review*, Defoe remarked, 'I know, what Mr. *Lock*, *Sidney* and others have said on this Head, and I must confess, I never thought their Systems fully answer'd—But I am arguing by my own Light, not other Mens; and therefore my Notions may be new. . . .'[2] Most critics have denied Defoe's claim to originality, treating him as a follower of Locke and a popularizer of his theories. To view him in this light is to see his resemblance to the major political theorist of the time, but many of Defoe's 'Revolution Maxims' seem to have been formulated before Locke's *Treatises* appeared in print.[3] Like Locke, Defoe was strongly influenced by the two main streams of political thought in England during the latter half of the seventeenth century: the doctrines of Hobbes and his disciples and those of their opponents, perhaps best represented by Richard Cumberland.[4] It was typical of Defoe's contemporaries to attempt a synthesis of these two views, and it is not surprising to find in Defoe's

---

by water as barbarous. He frequently satirized the superstition of mobs which punished women whose only sins were 'to have the Misfortune to be somewhat elderly'. See Lee, ii. 127; iii. 274–7; and *Political History of the Devil*, pp. 350, 376.

[1] Bk. iii, p. 10.   [2] iii. 429b.

[3] See, for example, *Reflections upon the Late Great Revolution* (1689), pp. 6, 36–62.

[4] Cumberland's arguments against Hobbes were given wide circulation by Pufendorf's extensive quotations from his writings and by the translations and abridgements of his disciples. See Samuel Pufendorf, *Of the Law of Nature and Nations*, trans. Basil Kennett (1703), pp. 54 (I. vi. 14), 90 n. 2 (II. ii. 9), 105 (II. iii. 13), 143–4 (VII. ii. 4); Samuel Parker, *A Demonstration of the Divine Authority of the Law of Nature, and of the Christian Religion* (1681), pp. iii–ix, xix, 17–35; and James Tyrrell, *A Brief Disquisition of the Law of Nature* (1693), especially sigs. A5–A6ᵛ, B3. See also Maurice Cranston, *John Locke* (1957), pp. 61–63; and W. von Leyden, ed., *Essays on the Law of Nature*, by John Locke (1954), pp. 14, 37–38, 66–71, 85–87.

political man a cross between Hobbes's wolf and Cumberland's sheep.

Credit for bringing the state of nature into seventeenth-century politics must be granted to Hobbes. The resulting state of nature was more nearly a description of government in savage society than either the Garden of Eden or the condition of the unregenerate. Beginning with man as a political abstraction, Hobbes argued that 'Men considered in meer, Nature ought to admit amongst themselves Equality'.[1] Such a proposition was acceptable to almost all contemporary writers on politics and economics, and it is probably the one statement of Hobbes which even his enemies did not dispute. Like Hobbes, Defoe also commenced with the state of nature and natural man, but his conclusions were somewhat different.

The basis for Defoe's theory of society was a belief in a divine right of property. If God had not given Adam control over the land and animals, man would be forced to expend all his energies in an individual struggle to survive. Property, there-fore, is essential to the existence of society:

Be fruitful, and multiply, and replenish the Earth, and subdue it— What is this but a Grant of Property—And a License to his Posterity to take Possession of every part of it—For by Vertue of this Grant, it was lawful, and doubtless is still, for any of *Adam's* Posterity to seize upon, and possess as his own, any part of the Creation of God, not inhabited or possess'd before—And Priority of Possession is a just Right of Property.[2]

Given this 'Grant of Property', man follows his social instinct and becomes a member of a community. Defoe contended that government was an 'Appendix of Nature' and that

... if twenty Men born in the dark, and that had never known Men or things, were set on Shore in an Island, where they had no body to imitate, and nothing to do but to live; the first thing they would apply to by the Light of Nature after Food, would be to settle Government among them.[3]

---

[1] Thomas Hobbes, *Tripos*, 3rd ed. (1684), p. 98.
[2] *Review*, iii. 430a. [3] Ibid., iii. 431a.

But without man's 'Dominion' over the earth and without property, government would be impossible.

Defoe did not regard man as a creature unfit for society as did Rousseau, but rather as a being for whom government was a natural law. Like so many of his contemporaries, even writers so different as Sir William Temple and Henry Sacheverell, Defoe argued that the family was the primary social unit.[1] In one of his last works, he attacked Hobbes's concept of the solitary natural man and the state of nature:

If we consider Mankind in his true natural State, we shall not see him as the Hobbists *would ridiculously insinuate, who imagine only Men of the Male-kind fighting with one another; on the contrary, we find Mankind Male and Female, and the most ardent appetites will then plainly appear to be a Fondness for their Women, and a Tenderness for their Off-spring, and this is even common to them with some Brutes; and therefore the* true State of Nature.[2]

Yet *Robert Drury's Journal*, the work in which this quotation appears, portrays a savage society which is continually disturbed by wars and violence. In spite of Defoe's attacks on Hobbes's lupine concept of humanity, he was strongly influenced by his ideas on human depravity. Thus if 'Reason and Nature' lead these people to a peaceful existence under ideal conditions, their 'Follies and Passions . . . lead them into Misery'.[3]

According to Defoe's theory, the primitive patriarchal state of nature gradually gave way to a period of violence. The picture which Defoe draws of the condition of the human race after the Flood is similar to Hobbes's state of nature in which man's life was 'nasty, brutish, and short':

We read of no considerable Wars indeed, but 'tis not to be doubted there were such Wars, or else it is to be understood that they liv'd (in common) a Life some what like the Brutes, the Strong devouring the Weak; for the Text says, *the whole Earth was fill'd with Violence,*

---

[1] See Temple, *Miscellanea* (1680), pp. 63–80; and Sacheverell, *The New Association* (1703), part II, sup., p. 7.

[2] *Madagascar: or, Robert Drury's Journal* (1729), p. xiii.

[3] Ibid., p. 336.

hunting and tearing one another in Pieces, either for Dominion or
for Wealth, either for Ambition or for Avarice, we know not well
which.[1]

Like Locke, Defoe distinguished between the peaceful 'state of
nature' and the 'state of war', which arose from human corruption and the absence of restraints upon freedom.

For Defoe, the state of nature applied only to that time in the
history of a society when government was under the head of the
family. Crime soon destroyed the security of this peaceful life,
and man abandoned patriarchal government to form the state:

> But *as* to wider Regions Nations spread,
> And weaker Numbers made the Great their Head,
> Eternal Feuds the Petty Lords invade,
> To *Lust and Crime*, by *Lust and Crime* betray'd;
> Necessity Confederate Heads Directs,
> And Power United, Power Expos'd Protects;
> The Nature of the Thing directs *the Mode*,
> And Government was born in *Publick Good*:
> *Safety* with *Right* and *Property* combines,
> And thus *Necessity* with Nature *joins*.[2]

In order to protect themselves, the people joined and formed
a government. But Defoe's political man never gives up his
freedom to rebel when his life is threatened. The 'great original'
of power in the state is always the people.

Although power remains with the people, the citizen volun-
teers to have his liberty restricted by his society:

> Laws are the just Restraint of wilder Sense,
> And Reason form'd them, for its own Defence:
> What tho' by Crime they're introduc'd at first,
> The Crime, not the Contrivance, shou'd be curst.[3]

Civil government, then, may be said to arise as a reasonable
solution to the existence of crime. Following the ideas of

---

[1] *Political History of the Devil*, p. 152.

[2] *Jure Divino*, bk. ii, p. 4. Defoe refers his reader to Samuel Pufendorf's
History of Europe for historical evidence, but Pufendorf's account is as brief
as Defoe's.   [3] Ibid., bk. v, p. 2.

Hobbes, Spinoza, and Algernon Sidney, Defoe argued that submission to law was the only endurable kind of slavery—a slavery to reason:

> The greatest Freedom Mankind e're obtained,
> Is to be *but from Doing ill* restrain'd.[1]

True freedom is not to be found in the state of nature but rather under law and government.

Defoe spoke of 'Crime' as the force which drove men into government, but he admitted that the particular reason was the 'Sense of Power Supream' which has always existed in certain 'vicious Men'.[2] This theory of the drive for power seems to be taken from Hobbes who regarded 'a perpetuall and restless desire of Power after power, that ceaseth onely in Death' as the strongest 'generall inclination of all mankind'.[3] Defoe adopted this concept for his view of the dangers of government:

> Nature has left *this Tincture in the Blood*,
> That all Men *would be Tyrants* if they cou'd:
> If they forbear their Neighbours to devour,
> 'Tis not for want of *Will*, but want *of Power*.[4]

Of course, in this passage Defoe was echoing his favourite lines from Rochester:

> Meerly for safety, after Fame we thirst,
> For all Men, wou'd be Cowards if they durst.[5]

Significantly enough, these are the lines which Shaftesbury attacked as immoral, for they suggest that man is primarily interested in power and that only after he has failed in his 'lust of Power' does he seek security in government.[6] Distrusting human goodness as much as Rochester, Defoe contended that the citizen must retain the right to protect himself from the magistrate who is always likely to be corrupted by his power.

---

[1] *A Hymn to the Mob* (1715), p. 13.   [2] *Jure Divino*, bk. v, p. 2.
[3] *Leviathan*, ed. A. R. Waller (1935), p. 63.
[4] Introduction, *Jure Divino*, p. i.
[5] John Wilmot, *Poems*, ed. Vivian de Sola Pinto (1953), p. 122, ll. 157–8.
[6] Anthony Cooper, Lord Shaftesbury, *Characteristics*, ed. John M. Robertson (1900), i. 79–81.

The magistrate is not a god; he is subject to the same temptations as the ordinary citizen:

> Mankind delights his Neighbours *to devour*,
> And is not fit to be supply'd with Power.[1]

Since the ruler of a state can so easily become the enemy of the
citizen, each person in the community must retain his right to
self-defence. All the followers of Cumberland and even Locke,
in his *Essays on the Law of Nature*, argued that Hobbes was
wrong in granting to man a right of self-defence. Man, they
contended, could use his reason in choosing an honourable
death before a dishonourable life. In proclaiming self-defence
as a law of nature as well as a right, Defoe was more radical
than even Hobbes:

> *The Laws of God*, as I can understand,
> Do never Laws of Nature countermand;
> Nature Commands, and 'tis Prescrib'd to Sense,
> For all Men to adhere to *Self-defence*:
> *Self-Preservation* is the only Law,
> That does *Involuntary Duty* Draw;
> It serves for Reason and Authority,
> And they'll defend themselves, *that know not why*.[2]

According to Defoe, the right of self-defence, like the idea of
government, was written in the hearts of all men. Advocates for
the theories of passive obedience and the divine right of kings
might argue against a right of self-defence, but during the
Glorious Revolution, when their own lives were threatened,
even they instinctively rebelled.

Such obvious truths as the right of self-defence are ignored
because many men have abandoned the rational self-interest
which led them to create society. For Defoe regarded self-love
as the true key to human nature:

> Men may *sometimes* by Subtilty and Slight
> *Oppose themselves*, and Sacrifice their Right;
> *But all's a Blast*, the empty Fraud's in vain,

---

[1] *Jure Divino*, bk. v, p. 18.   [2] Ibid., bk. iii, p. 10.

Int'rest Instructs, and all's restor'd again;
Self-Love's the Ground of all the things we do,
Which they *that talk on't least* do most pursue.[1]

The basis for all human activities in politics and economics, self-love is pictured as a kind of right reason. In discussing the corruption of English politics, Defoe merely remarked that mankind never changes:

> King *GEORGE'S* Servants are but Flesh and Blood any more than King *James* the Second's, or King *Charles* the Second's Servants were, and the same Flesh and Blood, perhaps, as all the Kings Servants that ever reign'd, have been; and that when they come to manage their own Interests, they act with the same Passion for their Profit, their Grandeur, their Faction, as other Men do, or have done, and perhaps will ever do in every Reign.[2]

Self-interest, then, is at least a predictable factor in all human beings living under the corrupt law of nature.

But Defoe never came to believe that an *ordre naturel* would change self-interest into universal good. The self-love which Defoe recognized as the centre of human action is unlike that which appears in the writings of Bishop Butler or Hutcheson, for it is balanced neither by benevolence nor a moral sense. Defoe attacked those merchants who refused to suspend their business during the plague at Marseilles, commenting sadly on the self-interest of mankind which places profit before the common good. Such examples of human corruption merely confirmed Defoe's arguments on the nature of man:

> *Self*, in a Word, governs the whole World; the present Race of Men all come into it. 'Tis the foundation of every prospect in Life, the beginning and end of our Actions; and where those Actions, at any Time, do not answer this End, they are so far eccentrick and out of square. 'Tis to move retrograde to the general System of Life; and to stand as it were by ourselves.[3]

Lacking Mandeville's faith in the successful operation of the

---

[1] *Jure Divino*, bk. iv, p. 8. See Defoe's discussion of La Rochefoucauld in *The Commentator*, No. 12 (8 February 1720).
[2] *The Conduct of Robert Walpole* (1717), p. 52.
[3] Lee, iii. 346.

human hive, Defoe searched for solutions to the problem of self-interest in the power of the state to make laws which would force self-interest to work for the common good and in the spiritual power of religion.

An ardent propagandist for reformation of manners and morals, Defoe frequently satirized the swearing, drunkenness, and sexual licence of his age. Few writers enjoyed paradox as much as Defoe; few subjects were more paradoxical than the discrepancy between the actual state of eighteenth-century society and its rational ideals. An absurd penal code, the corruptions of Augustan politics and the condition of the poor furnished ample material for the Christian moralist, but Defoe was aware that an appeal to reason was the more effective plea for his contemporaries. As a result, he developed his ideas on natural law more as a weapon of social satire than as a systematic doctrine. We will see in the next chapter on *Robinson Crusoe*, however, that Defoe was also fascinated by some of the more abstract implications of the laws of nature.

II

ROBINSON CRUSOE AND THE STATE OF NATURE

I

> . . . 'tis a little wonderful, and what I believe few People have thought much upon, (*viz.*) the strange multitude of little Things necessary in the Providing, Producing, Curing, Dressing, Making and Finishing this one Article of Bread.
>
> I that was reduced to a meer State of Nature, found this to my daily Discouragement. . . .
>
> DEFOE, *The Life and Surprising Adventures of Robinson Crusoe*[1]

WHEN Crusoe remarks that he is in a 'State of Nature', Defoe's audience must have recognized both the aptness and the ambiguity of this statement. By 1719, when *Robinson Crusoe* was first published, the problem of defining natural man and the state of nature had been the subject of considerable speculation. Arthur Lovejoy suggested that there were three principle meanings for the term 'state of nature' in the eighteenth century. It could be used in an historical or anthropological sense to refer to the 'primeval condition of man'; in a 'cultural sense' to refer to a stage of society in which the arts and sciences had not yet progressed beyond a few primitive tools; or in a political sense to indicate the relationships between men before the creation of government.[2] Although there are some notable omissions, Lovejoy's triad is a convenient classification for a discussion of *Robinson Crusoe*, for Defoe was not only delineating

---

[1] In the Shakespeare Head Edition of the *Novels and Selected Writings of Daniel Defoe* (1927), i. 135. Subsequent references to this edition of Defoe's writings will be cited as Shakespeare Head ed.

[2] Arthur Lovejoy, 'The supposed Primitivism of Rousseau's *Discourses on Inequality*' in *Essays in the History of Ideas* (1948), pp. 14–15.

the condition of man in the state of nature but also the cultural and political evolution which, by transforming the state of nature, created civilization and government.

Lovejoy's scheme omits two important ideas. He makes no mention of the theological implications of man's natural state—the idea that every man has a law of reason written in his heart by God. In this sense, the state of nature refers to any condition which is governed by the laws of nature. This is what Crusoe means when he remarks that before his religious conversion he 'acted like a meer Brute from the Principles of Nature'.[1] Secondly Lovejoy does not explain that in the seventeenth and eighteenth centuries, discussions of the primitive state of man almost always commenced with the image of an isolated being, abstracted from society and religion. Three opinions on the solitary natural man were current in Defoe's day. Some writers believed that the isolated natural man might, through the use of his reason, achieve the same moral and intellectual condition as the human being raised in society. Others, following certain hints in Lucretius, suggested that he would be savage and brutal but have greater freedom and happiness and fewer vices than civilized man. The majority of writers, however, argued that man was a social animal, that the bestial life of the solitary savage was insecure, and that so far from being happy, the isolated natural man lived in constant fear of death. Although most modern critics have regarded Crusoe as an embodiment of the enterprising, fearless economic man, Crusoe clearly belongs to the third category. He survives his solitude, but he is always afraid, always cautious. Defoe recognized the benefits of the state of nature, but he believed that the freedom and purity of Crusoe's island were minor advantages compared to the comfort and security of civilization.

[1] *Robinson Crusoe*, i. 101.

II

> Man is a creature so formed for society, that it may not
> only be said that it is not good for him to be alone, but
> 'tis really impossible he should be alone.
>
> DEFOE, *Serious Reflections of Robinson Crusoe*[1]

IN 1708, the year that Alexander Selkirk was rescued from the
island of Juan Fernandez and eleven years before the appearance of *Robinson Crusoe*, Abu ibn al-Tufail's *The Improvement
of Human Reason*, a narrative of another solitary, was translated
into English. Robinson Crusoe was to replace both Tufail's
hero, Hai Ibn Yokdhan, and Selkirk as the paradigm of the
isolated natural man, but for Alexander Pope, writing in 1719,
Selkirk and Yokdhan were still the best examples.[2] Yokdhan's
story was widely read in an earlier Latin translation, and in
1702 he appeared in a dialogue with the Turkish Spy as a
spokesman for natural rights and freedom.[3] He was entirely
a child of nature. While yet a baby, Yokdhan was wafted by the
waves to a desert island, where he was suckled by a doe and
reared as an animal. After the death of his foster-mother, he
rejected his brute existence and began to examine his world and
its principles. By the use of his reason Yokdhan eventually discovers the secrets of life, hell, heaven, and God. A religious
hermit who arrives at the island teaches Yokdhan how to speak
and discovers to his astonishment that what Yokdhan has
learned from nature is the same as the knowledge contained in
the *Koran*. After a time, they leave the island to visit the world,
where Yokdhan is disappointed to find everyone pursuing
worldly pleasures and wealth.

Parallels with the life of Crusoe are remarkable./The hero is
completely isolated for more than twenty years, dresses in
animal skins, and indulges in religious speculations. He even has
a 'Vision of the Angelic World' in the manner of Defoe's hero;

[1] p. 12. Defoe is probably echoing John Norris's essay 'Of Solitude'.
See *A Collection of Miscellanies*, 3rd ed. (1699), pp. 125-8.

[2] Alexander Pope, *Correspondence*, ed. George Sherburn (1956), ii. 13.

[3] See *Memoirs for the Curious*, i (1701), 47-50.

so that one is led to speculate as to whether or not Defoe knew
the story of Yokdhan. Yet so far from being the 'idea' of *Robinson
Crusoe* as one writer has suggested, it is almost the complete
reverse.[1]

'He', wrote Aristotle, 'who is unable to live in society, or who
has no need because he is sufficient for himself, must be either
a beast or a god.'[2] Some critics have decided that Robinson
Crusoe is indeed almost godlike, that he is an economic super-
man, enjoying his exploitation of the resources of the island and
regretting his solitude only when he needs a helper in his labours.
Such a view probably did not occur to Defoe. Commenting on
Crusoe's life through the mask of his narrator, Defoe remarked:
'Here is invincible patience recommended under the worst of
misery, indefatigable application and undaunted resolution
under the greatest and most discouraging circumstances.'[3]
Behind this statement lies Aristotle's view of man as a social
animal, for whom loneliness was a terrifying condition. Not very
long after Defoe's death, Rousseau eulogized the happiness of
the solitary savage. But for Defoe, solitude was 'a rape upon
human nature',[4] the worst of all punishments for his erring hero.

Cut off from the world, Crusoe's mind is dominated by fear.
'This bold man', Giraudoux observed, 'was constantly trembling
with fear, and it was thirteen years before he dared to recon-
noitre all his island.'[5] Upon reaching land, the sole survivor of
a terrible shipwreck, Crusoe might be expected to express some
joy at his salvation from the sea; instead his first reaction is
panic:

> I had a dreadful Deliverance: For I was wet, had no Clothes to
> shift me, nor any thing either to eat or drink to comfort me, neither
> did I see any Prospect before me, but that of perishing with Hunger,
> or being devour'd by wild Beasts; and that which was particularly
> afflicting to me was that I had no Weapon either to hunt and kill

[1] See A. C. R. Pastor, *The Idea of Robinson Crusoe* (1930), p. 1.
[2] *Politics*, *Works*, trans. Benjamin Jowett (1952), x, 1253[a].
[3] *Serious Reflections*, p. xii.   [4] Ibid., p. 6.
[5] Jean Giraudoux, *Suzanne and the Pacific*, trans. Ben Redman (1923),
p. 225.

any Creature for my Sustenance, or to defend my self against any other Creature that might desire to kill me for theirs: In a Word, I had nothing about me but a Knife, a Tobacco-pipe, and a little Tobacco in a Box, this was all my Provision, and threw me into terrible Agonies of Mind, that for a while I run about like a Madman; Night coming upon me, I began with a heavy Heart to consider what would be my Lot if there were any ravenous Beasts in that Country, seeing at Night they always come abroad for their Prey.[1]

Climbing into a tree for the night, Crusoe contemplates what he regards as his inevitable fate—destruction by violence or starvation.

Such a reaction may not seem unlikely under the circumstances, but Crusoe returns to the memory of this scene throughout the work, dwelling on and embellishing the description of his fear. He tells the reader: 'I ran about the Shore, wringing my Hands and beating my Head and Face, exclaiming at my Misery, and crying out, I was undone.'[2] When he sees the English captain in despair at being abandoned on the island by his mutinous crew, Crusoe is reminded of his emotions when he first arrived: 'How I gave myself over for lost; How wildly I look'd round me: What dreadful Apprehensions I had: and how I lodg'd in the Tree all Night for fear of being devour'd by wild Beasts.'[3] In his journal, he recalls his despair and fear of starvation, recounting how, instead of searching for food and shelter, he could only think about the necessities he lacked: 'Food, House, Clothes, Weapon, or Place to fly to.'[4] During these first hours on the island, Crusoe lacks all the resources of mind which are usually associated with his adventure.

Fear, Defoe was clearly saying, is the dominant passion of a man in Crusoe's condition. His isolation identifies him with the state of nature which precedes society, a condition in which man could live alone not because he was godlike, but because he was bestial. Probably the best contemporary description of man in his natural state was provided by Samuel Pufendorf in his *De*

---

[1] *Robinson Crusoe*, i. 52.   [2] Ibid., i. 78.   [3] Ibid., ii. 43.
[4] Ibid., i. 79.

Jure Naturae et Gentium and *De Officio Hominis et Civis*. The 'ingenious Puffendorf', as Defoe called him,[1] pictured the natural state as 'opposed to a life improved by the industry of men'—a life which must have been filled with continual fears and doubts and 'more wretched than that of any wild beast'.[2]

Pufendorf's description of natural man born into a state of isolation loosely parallels Crusoe's condition:

Now to form in our Minds some Image of this Natural State, as such as it would be if destitute of all Arts and Assistances either invented by Men, or reveal'd by GOD, we must fancy a Man thrown at a venture into the World, and then left entirely to himself without receiving any farther Help or Benefit from others, than his bare Nativity; we must likewise suppose him to be furnish'd with no larger Endowments of Body or Mind, than such as we can now discover in men antecedent to all Culture and Information; and lastly, we must take it for granted, that he is not foster'd under the peculiar Care and Concern of Heaven. The Condition of such a Person could not prove otherwise than extreamly miserable, whether he were thus cast upon the Earth in Infancy, or in Maturity of Stature and of Strength. If an Infant, he could not but have sadly perish'd, unless some Brute Creature had by a kind of Miracle offer'd its Duggs for his Support; and then he must necessarily have imbib'd a fierce and savage Temper, under the Nursery and Education of Beasts. If in Perfection of Limbs and Size, we must however conceive him Naked, able to utter but an inarticulate Sound, . . . amaz'd and startled at the things about him, and even at his own Being.[3]

Although such a passage may, at first, seem more applicable to the life of Hai Ibn Yokdhan than to Defoe's hero, actually it reveals precisely the same attitude toward isolation which appears in the *Serious Reflections*. Certainly Crusoe has an education and considers himself under the special care of heaven, but like Pufendorf's abstraction, he is the ordinary man separated from the rest of humanity and forced to struggle for survival in a natural environment.

[1] *The Interest of the Several Princes and States of Europe* (1698), p. 13.
[2] *De Officio Hominis et Civis*, trans. Frank Moore (1927), ii. 89 (II. i. 4).
[3] *Law of Nature*, p. 79 (II. ii. 2).

Pufendorf described how this natural man would react. First he would feel hunger and thirst; then he would search eagerly for the means to satisfy his needs. After satisfying these instincts, he would fall asleep among the trees. Crusoe does precisely the same thing, quenching his thirst and falling asleep in spite of his fears. But fear does not disappear with sleep. It remains the dominant emotion of natural man:

What a wretched Creature we should at last behold! A mute and an ignoble Animal, Master of no Powers or Capacities any farther than to pluck up the Herbs and Roots that grow about him; to gather the Fruits which he did not plant; to quench his Thirst at the first River, or Fountain or Ditch, that he finds out in his way; to creep into a Cave for Shelter from the Injuries of Weather, or to cover over his Body with Moss and Grass and Leaves; Thus would he pass a heavy Life in most tedious Idleness; would tremble at every Noise, and be scar'd at the approach of any of his Fellow Creatures, till at last his miserable days were concluded by the Extremity of Hunger or Thirst, or by the Fury of a ravenous Beast.[1]

Like Pufendorf's abstraction, Crusoe eventually finds a cave to hide in and surrounds his shelter with an impenetrable wall of stakes. He fears every noise, in spite of his failure to discover the wild beasts which he imagines are in possession of the island. After one of his few attempts at exploration, Crusoe mentions how happy he is to return to the security of his home. When he decides to make another entrance to his cave, he is seized with a sudden anxiety. 'I was not perfectly easy at lying so open', he says, 'for as I had manag'd my self before, I was in a perfect Enclosure, whereas now I thought I lay expos'd'.[2] He fears the attack of some enemy although he admits that he has not seen anything on the island more dangerous than a goat. Such a reaction might be considered normal enough during his first few days on the island, but Crusoe still lives in fear a year after his arrival.

In the *Serious Reflections* Crusoe remarks that an 'eminent poet tells us that all courage is fear'.[3] The poet is Rochester, and

---

[1] *Law of Nature*, p. 78 (II. i. 8).   [2] *Robinson Crusoe*, i. 118.
[3] *Serious Reflections*, p. 25.

the passage is significant, for it deduces all the passions from the ruling passion of fear. Rochester compared the wisdom of animals, who only fight for love or hunger to man who fights from fear:

> For fear he armes, and is of Armes afraid,
> By fear, to fear, successively betray'd
> Base fear, the source whence his best passion[s] came,
> His boasted Honor, and his dear bought Fame.
>
> . . . . . .
>
> Look to the bottom, of his vast design,
> Wherein *Mans* Wisdom, Pow'r, and Glory joyn;
> The good he acts, the ill he does endure,
> 'Tis all for fear, to make himself secure.[1]

Crusoe quotes a large part of the *Satyr Against Mankind* as well as sections of Creech's translation of Lucretius. The combination is significant, for Lucretius's discussion of man in the state of nature formed the basis for Rochester's theories as well as those of Hobbes.

Although Rochester and Hobbes argued that man in his natural state would be divided by his lust after power and his fears, most philosophers contended that fear was the dominant passion. Montesquieu's brief view of natural man in his *Spirit of the Laws* was approximately the same as Pufendorf's:

> Man in a state of nature would have the faculty of knowing, before he had acquired any knowledge. Plain it is that his first ideas would not be of a speculative nature; he would think of the preservation of his being, before he would investigate its origin. Such a man would feel nothing in himself at first but impotency and weakness; his fears and apprehensions would be excessive; as appears from instances (were there any necessity of proving it) of savages found in forests, trembling at the motion of a leaf, and flying from every shadow.[2]

The reference which Montesquieu supplies for what he obviously regards as a self-evident statement is to a 'savage' found

[1] 'Satyr Against Mankind', *Poems*, ed. Vivian de Sola Pinto (1953), p. 122.
[2] Trans. Thomas Nugent (1949), p. 4.

in the forests of Hanover and brought over to England in 1726. The arrival of this natural man, Peter the Wild Boy, in England produced a flood of anonymous pamphlets and poems and one long work, *Mere Nature Delineated*, by Defoe. Most of the pamphlets contained some form of satire on Walpole or the court; all of them suggested ideas on primitivism which were more typical of the period after Rousseau than the time of *Gulliver's Travels*. Later in the century, Rousseau's British disciple, Lord Monboddo, used Peter's case to illustrate man's happy animalism in the state of nature, but his exposition, while clearly more serious, offered few ideas which had not been suggested when Peter first arrived in England. In the *Manifesto of Lord Peter* the Wild Boy is seen searching for a wife who is free from the evil influences of a civilized education 'which may have corrupted the Simplicity of Nature';[1] while the narrator of *It Cannot Rain But It Pours* tells of the rumour that

. . . the new Sect of Herb-eaters intend to follow him into the Fields. . . . And that there are many of them now thinking of turning their Children into Woods to Graze with the Cattle, in hopes to raise a healthy and moral Race, refin'd from the Corruptions of this Luxurious World.[2]

In reply to these pamphlets and their half-joking suggestions that by creating governments and erecting cities man had destroyed the purity of his feral state, Defoe issued his *Mere Nature Delineated*. The title suggests that the work is related to William Wollaston's *Religion of Nature Delineated*, which probably antagonized Defoe by attempting to construct a system of natural morality. But although Defoe unquestionably objected to some of Wollaston's premises, he would have been in complete agreement with Wollaston's attack on those philosophers who believed that men could attain virtue by following nature. Like Defoe, Wollaston praised civilization for elevating man's reason above his passions, remarking that if there were another

[1] (London, 1726), p. 9. See also David Lewis ed., *Miscellaneous Poems* (1726), p. 305.
[2] (1726), p. 8.

Flood, only the 'natural fools' would return to the woods. He also argued that man was a social creature and that '. . . it is certain that absolute and perpetual solitude has something in it very disagreeable and hideous'.[1] These, however, are ideas which Defoe had formulated long before Wollaston's book appeared in 1722. It must be concluded that Defoe merely adapted the title of a popular and controversial work to draw attention to his own study of a very different subject: the problems raised by the discovery of a man in his natural state.

Defoe's observations on Peter are important because they show his disagreement with the central moral of Hai Ibn Yokdhan's life: that '. . . nature of its meer undirected inclination guided mankind to make the best choice of things, and rejecting the pleasing objects of sence, led him to choose vertue by a meer propensity of will without instruccion or example'.[2] In regard to Peter's condition, Defoe remarked that the Wild Boy was 'passive, weak, foolish, as well as wild', not strong and fearless as Hobbes suggested natural man would be.[3] Defoe speculated on this being in a 'State of Meer Nature' wondering whether he could reason or form ideas without the power of language. The main trouble with Peter, Defoe concluded, was that he lacked any kind of education or civilization. Comparing him to a deaf girl who had learned how to speak at the age of fourteen, Defoe remarked that the natural man was 'a plain coarse Piece of Work', and that without some kind of learning a knowledge of language or religion would be impossible.[4]

Both Crusoe and Peter the Wild Boy were in a natural state because they were solitaries, entirely outside of society. By the end of the eighteenth century, Zimmermann was to write a book praising some kinds of solitude as remedies for many problems of the mind and heart, but even he regarded absolute isolation with distrust. The possibility of a *dementia ex separatione* was clearly perceived by writers of the seventeenth and eighteenth centuries. Stories of men isolated for long periods, such as that

---

[1] (1722), pp. 67, 107. [2] *Compleat English Gentleman*, p. 111.
[3] *Mere Nature Delineated* (1726), p. 8. [4] Ibid., p. 68.

of Pedro Serrano in Garcilaso de la Vega's *Royal Commentaries of the Yncas*, parallel Crusoe's adventure in many ways, but after three years on his island Serrano said that 'he would have been glad to end his misery by death'.[1] Serrano was almost reduced to the condition of an animal; so that when a companion finally came to the island, he could not believe Serrano was a human being. Because isolation was regarded with such horror, pirates often assumed that marooning a victim on an uninhabited island would be worse punishment than death. After only five days alone, Richard Norwood, one of the early settlers of Bermuda, had sunk into despair:

> This five days seemed to me the most tedious and miserable time that I ever underwent in all my life, yea, though I had had experience of sundry difficulties, dangers, and hard conditions before; yet till then I never seemed to understand what misery was; yet I had victuals sufficient, only I seemed banished from human society and knew not how long it might last. Yet at other times I was apt to retire myself much from company, but at this time I thought it was one of the greatest punishments in the world, yea, I thought it was one of the greatest punishments in hell, and the sense and apprehension of it made me to think of hell as of hell indeed, a condition most miserable.[2]

Norwood, like Serrano, thought that he would rather suffer any torture than be deprived of human society, but Serrano and several others endured this loneliness for many years.

Perhaps the best example of this ability to endure loneliness was Alexander Selkirk. Although he experienced some fear, Selkirk 'came at last to conquer all the inconveniences of his solitude, and to be very easy'.[3] Around Selkirk's life two myths have arisen which seem to have little factual basis. The first concerned Steele's statement that Selkirk '. . . frequently bewailed his return to the world, which could not . . . with all its

---

[1] Trans. Clements Markham (1869), i. 44.

[2] *The Journal of Richard Norwood*, ed. Wesley Craven and Walter Hayward (1945), p. 54. For a modern study of isolation see A. L. Singh and Robert Zingg, *Wolf Children and Feral Man* (1942), pp. 247–9.

[3] Woodes Rogers, *A Cruising Voyage Round the World*, in Defoe, *Romances*, Dent ed., iii. 322.

enjoyments, restore him to the tranquillity of his solitude'.[1] The
second is the idea that Selkirk had slipped back into animalism
and lost the use of speech.[2] Steele's version turned Selkirk's
experience into something not very different from the life of
Hai Ibn Yokdhan; whereas followers of Rousseau, like Monboddo, pointed to Selkirk as proof that when returned to the
state of nature, man quickly reverts to his bestial origins.

Defoe adapted neither of these myths. From time to time
Crusoe has a certain nostalgia for the primitive conditions of his
island, but never does he suggest that he would like to return
to his solitary state of nature. In the *Serious Reflections* Defoe
repeated the story of Saint Hilarion, who spent his life in the
desert only to discover that a simple labourer, living in the midst
of a city, had led a more holy life than he:

There is no need of a wilderness to wander among wild beasts, no
necessity of a cell on the top of a mountain, or a desolate island in the
sea; if the mind be confined, if the soul be truly master of itself,
all is safe; for it is certainly and effectually master of the body, and
what signify retreats, especially a forced retreat as mine was?[3]

Defoe probably realized that Crusoe's isolation on his island
was almost the same as the isolation of the desert fathers. Living
in a cave, dividing his life between work and prayer, seeing
visions, Crusoe seems not very different from a religious hermit.
But Defoe rejected this idea by pointing to his hero's misery
and to his inability to leave the island. Crusoe insists that he
could 'enjoy much more solitude in the middle of the greatest
collection of mankind in the world' than in twenty-eight years
of isolation.[4] Crusoe is not a saint. Charles Kingsley called him

[1] Richard Steele, *The Englishman*, in Defoe, *Romances*, Dent ed., iii.
328.
[2] See Isaac James, *Providence Displayed* (1800), p. 100; and James
Burnet, Lord Monboddo, *Of the Origin and Progress of Language*, 2nd ed.
(1774), i. 198.
[3] *Serious Reflections*, p. 6.
[4] The comparison between Selkirk's isolation and that of the desert
fathers was apparent to Captain Edward Cooke, who urged his readers to
peruse the 'Lives of ancient Anchorites, who spent many years in the
Deserts of *Thebaida* in *Egypt*' if they wanted to learn about the moral benefits

a 'Protestant monk', but this is paradoxical.[1] Crusoe's real life
was to be lived in the world, following his calling, not on the
island where much of his time was spent in hiding from
imaginary enemies.

Although Crusoe's manufacturing, farming, and building
are given most space in the novel, much of his time is devoted
to self-defence:

> The anxiety of my circumstances there, I can assure you, was
> such for a time as was very unsuitable to heavenly meditations, and
> even when that was got over, the frequent alarms from the savages
> put the soul sometimes to such extremities of fear and horror, that
> all manner of temper was lost, and I was no more fit for religious
> exercises than a sick man is fit for labour.[2]

Crusoe lives in a 'brutal solitude' and, like Pufendorf's natural
man, leads a life of 'perpetual doubt and danger'.[3] Pufendorf
described such an existence as being worse than that of a beast.
Nothing can be considered secure, and within the soul the
passions rule instead of reason. Lacking the aid of his fellow
man and forced to meet every enemy alone, the isolated natural
man passes his life in continual expectation of destruction.[4]
Crusoe is rescued from this condition by his tools, the symbols
of learning, the arts, society, and that civilization which is the
reverse of man's natural state. But as soon as he discovers the
footprint in the sand, Crusoe returns to his original state in
which fear rules every aspect of life.

'O what ridiculous Resolution Men take', says Crusoe, 'when
possess'd with Fear! It deprives them of the Use of those Means
which Reason offers for their Relief.'[5] Ruled by his passions,
Crusoe thinks of destroying everything which might indicate to

of isolation instead of wasting their time on a 'downright Sailor, whose only
Study was how to support himself, during his Confinement, and all his
Conversation with Goats'. *A Voyage to the South Sea* (1712), II. xix.
   [1] Introduction, *The Surprising Adventures of Robinson Crusoe* (1868),
p. xxii.   [2] *Serious Reflections*, p. 7.
   [3] Defoe, *An Historical Account of the Voyages and Adventures of Sir
Walter Raleigh* (1719), p. 44.
   [4] *De Officio Hominis et Civis*, ii. 90–93 (II. i. 7–11).
   [5] *Robinson Crusoe*, i. 184.

the savage who made that single footprint the possibility of some inhabitant on the island. He contemplates letting his goats run loose, digging up his corn fields, and even destroying his beloved cave and enclosure. Searching desperately for some means of defence, Crusoe forgets the consolation which religion offered him. Recalling these emotions from the safety of his study in England, he moralizes on the senselessness of his behaviour:

Thus Fear of Danger is ten thousand Times more terrifying than Danger it self, when apparent to the Eyes; and we find the Burthen of Anxiety greater by much, than the Evil which we are anxious about. . . .[1]

Crusoe was incapable of such moralizing on the island, for he passed most of his time attempting to ensure his safety. The impassable wood is now made ten feet thick, and after he has completed his fortification, Crusoe hides himself in his cave, afraid to leave, living 'in the constant Snare of the *Fear of Man*'.[2]

Crusoe remarks on the effect which his fear has upon his efforts at improving the conditions of his life: 'the Frights I had been in about these Savage Wretches, and the Concern I had been in for my own Preservation, had taken off the Edge of my Invention for my own Conveniences.'[3] Instead of making beer and providing for his comforts, Crusoe is forced to abandon even his most simple improvements. Defoe's concept is the same as that contained in one of the best-known passages from Hobbes's *Leviathan* describing the state of nature:

In such condition, there is no place for Industry; because the fruit thereof is uncertain: and consequently no Culture of the Earth; no Navigation, nor use of the commodities that may be imported by Sea; no commodius Building; no Instruments of moving, and removing such things as require much force; no Knowledge of the face of the Earth; no account of Time; no Arts; no Letters; no Society; and which is worst of all, continuall feare, and danger of violent death; And the life of man, solitary, poore, nasty, brutish, and short.[4]

Defoe, like Pufendorf, would have objected that such a picture

[1] Ibid., i. 184.   [2] Ibid., i. 189.   [3] Ibid., i. 194.
[4] p. 84.

could only apply to a society of solitary males, but this is precisely Crusoe's condition. Nor is this state of war a matter of a few days or the length of time required to fight a battle; it is rather a continual state of mind. Crusoe is no longer able to perfect his bread or invent a new type of grindstone; all his labour is directed to the task of preserving his life. Looking back, Crusoe is amused at the time and energy which he devoted to works of defence 'on the Account of the Print of a Man's Foot which I had seen; for as yet I never saw any human Creature come near the Island'.[1] But this is written from the safety of Crusoe's study in England. While he is on the island, he is unable to achieve this objectivity about his fears.

Crusoe recalls with longing the happiness of the first two years on the island, comparing them to 'the Life of Anxiety, Fear and Care' which have plagued him since his discovery of the cannibals.[2] And he rationalizes that the state of fear which these savages have induced in him is enough to justify his slaughtering them. 'It was Self-preservation in the highest Degree', he remarks, 'to deliver myself from this Death of a Life, and was acting in my own Defence, as much as if they were actually assaulting me.'[3] Only the arrival of Friday relieves him from his care and returns him to the life of peace and industry. With the coming of social life, man gladly abandons his isolation and enters the comparative security of the social state of nature.

III

... great part of the world, ... is resolved into the lowest degeneracy of human nature, I mean, the savage life; where the chief end of life seems to be merely to eat and drink, that is to say, to get their food, just as the brutal life is employed. ...

DEFOE, *Serious Reflections of Robinson Crusoe*[4]

ROUSSEAU once observed that although philosophers had often written about the state of nature, none had gone back far enough

---

[1] *Robinson Crusoe*, i. 188.   [2] Ibid., i. 227.   [3] Ibid., i. 231.
[4] p. 107.

in the history of mankind to discover it. But for both Defoe and Locke the state of nature was, more or less, theoretical and always implied a level of civilization beyond that associated with the savages of Africa and America. Leo Strauss remarked that for Locke 'an example of men who are in the state of nature under the law of nature would . . . be an elite among the English colonists in America rather than the wild Indians'.[1] Crusoe fits this role better than Friday, but although Crusoe was a useful abstraction for political theorists and economists of the next two centuries, examples of savage life continued to have the same appeal of authenticity which they had for seventeenth-century writers. Hobbes pointed to the American Indian as an illustration of natural man living under absolute monarchy, while with equal evidence from contemporary voyage literature Locke argued that the lives of these savages showed that man was naturally free. There is much about savages, cannibals, and pagans in Defoe's writings. Some passages seem to praise their primitive innocence and adherence to the laws of nature. But Defoe never abandoned the ideals of Christianity and civilization. Defoe's savages are only noble when they reflect ironically upon some corrupt aspect of European civilization. For the most part, his picture of the savage represents the depths to which human nature can fall when deprived of the benefits of European religion and culture.

Friday comes to Crusoe's island as a naked cannibal. He has eaten his meat uncooked and unsalted; he worships his God, Benamuckee, and believes that all creatures worship him. Yet Friday is easily converted to Christianity. He dresses in the ill-fitting clothes which Crusoe provides for him and learns to eat his meat cooked, to farm and to accomplish all the tasks which Crusoe had formerly performed for himself. Unlike Crusoe, Friday has almost all the virtues: gratitude, honesty, and courage. He is the perfect natural man. But he abandons the state of nature for the advantages of civilization. From the moment he accepts Crusoe as his master, he surrenders every

[1] *Natural Right and History* (1953), p. 230.

uncivilized characteristic, even his distaste for salt. Instead of reverting to the life of a savage, Crusoe remakes the paradigm of the noble savage into a civilized man.

Defoe's ideas must be understood in the context of contemporary attitudes towards the savage. When Montaigne decided to praise the cannibal as the true natural man, there was a strong suggestion of paradox in his arguments. He was not concerned with reason as a law of nature, but with nature as the true law of reason:

> Those people are wild in the sense in which we call wild the fruits that Nature has produced by herself and in her ordinary progress; whereas in truth it is those we have altered artificially and diverted from the common order, that we should rather call wild. In the first we still see, in full life and vigour, the genuine and most natural and useful virtues and properties, which we have bastardized in the latter, and only adapted to please our corrupt taste.[1]

Although Montaigne's subject was the natives of the Caribbean Sea, his real focus was on Europe. Such comparisons between the corruptions of western civilization and the virtues of the savage life became increasingly more popular during the seventeenth century.

Some writers even began to suggest that the savages of the newly discovered lands might be free from the sin of Adam; that since many savages did not work and wore no clothes at all, they might be under a different dispensation. Aphra Behn, writing of the same natives whom Raleigh had eulogized, suggested that the lives of the natives of Guiana resembled man's existence before the Fall:

> ... these people represented to me an absolute idea of the first state of innocence, before man knew how to sin: And 'tis most evident and plain, that simple Nature is the most harmless, inoffensive and virtuous mistress. It is she alone, if she were permitted, that better instructs the world, than all the inventions of man: religion would here but destroy that tranquillity they possess by ignorance; and laws would but teach them to know offences, of which they now have

---

[1] 'Of Cannibals', *Essays*, trans. E. J. Trechmann (1950), i. 205.

no notion. . . . They have a native justice, which knows no fraud; and they understand no vice, or cunning, but when they are taught by the white men.[1]

Transferring his attention to Madagascar, another author, Walter Hammond, attempted to prove that the Malagasy had escaped all the sins and vices which trade and civilization had brought to Europe. In defence of their nakedness he remarked, 'It is our own luxurious effeminacy, that has stripped us out of our natural simplicity.'[2] These encomiums of natural simplicity invariably contrasted the luxury of Europe with the simplicity of man's natural state.

With Shaftesbury the concept of man's natural goodness became part of a systematic philosophy which was to dominate eighteenth-century thought. Ignoring or denying the often unflattering accounts of the Indians, he identified the virtues of the savages with those of the Scythians, whose manner of living had often served Roman writers with points of contrast with their civilization. Shaftesbury recommended the followers of Hobbes to observe the lives of the noble savage if they wished a refutation of their theories:

One would imagine that if they turned their eye towards remote countries (of which they affect so much to speak) they should search for that simplicity of manners and innocence of behaviour which has been often known among savages ere they were corrupted by our commerce, and, by sad example, instructed in all kinds of treachery and inhumanity.[3]

Defoe was undoubtedly familiar with the primitivism of Shaftesbury and his followers. No one reading *Robinson Crusoe* could be unaware of the new current of thought. But there can be no question that many of Defoe's contemporaries saw much in Crusoe's relation to the cannibals and to Friday which Defoe never intended.

[1] *The Royal Slave*, in *The Novels of Mrs. Aphra Behn*, ed. Ernest Baker (1913), p. 3.
[2] Walter Hammond, *A Paradox*, in *Harleian Miscellany* (1810), xi. 536.
[3] *Characteristics*, i. 226.

Although he did not have the opportunity to expatiate on the ideals of primitivism before writing his novels and long didactic works, Defoe occasionally referred to the moral probity of savages even in his early pamphlets and poems. In attacking the English for their drunkenness, he remarked ironically that the '. . . Pleasure of it seems to be so secretly hid, that wild Heathen Nations know nothing of the matter; 'tis only to be discover'd by the wise people of these *Northern* Countries'.[1] And in a similar vein he suggested that if man would ever be forced to return to a stage of society in which all his efforts would have to be expended in hunting for his food, he might at least have the compensation of escaping from drinking and other civilized vices.[2]

But Defoe's real interest in primitivism commenced with *Robinson Crusoe* and continued for the next ten years. In a study of Raleigh, Defoe praised the inhabitants of Guiana as 'a Sensible, Sociable People', who would welcome English colonization.[3] A few years later, the hero of Defoe's *Life and Adventures of the Famous Captain Singleton* praised the virtues of the tribes he encountered in his journey across Africa. At one point in the story, he and his men come upon a tribe which has never seen white men before. Singleton describes these natives as 'the civillest and most friendly People that we met with at all, and mightily pleased with us'.[4] But the closer Singleton and his party come to civilization, the fiercer become the savages. Near the coast, they meet

. . . a more fierce and politick People than those we had met with before; not so easily terrified with our Arms as those, and not so ignorant, as to give their Provisions and Corn for our little Toys, such as I had said before our Artificer made; but as they had frequently traded and conversed with the *Europeans* on the Coast . . . they were the less ignorant, and the less fearful. . . .[5]

[1] 'The Poor Man's Plea' in *The Shortest Way with the Dissenters*, Shakespeare Head ed., p. 8.
[2] *Review*, iii. 454–6.
[3] *Historical Account of Sir Walter Raleigh*, p. 44.
[4] Shakespeare Head ed., p. 131.   [5] Ibid., p. 150.

The implication of this statement is unmistakable: the European makes the natives avaricious, fierce, and suspicious by corrupting their innocence.

This becomes a familiar theme in Defoe's subsequent works. The pirate, Captain Roberts, finds that the natives at Calabar refuse to trade with him and his vicious crew, providing Captain Johnson, Defoe's narrator, with an opportunity to moralize on this:

Indication that these poor Creatures, in the narrow Circumstances they were in, and without the Light of the Gospel, or the Advantages of an Education, have, notwithstanding, such a moral innate Honesty, as would upbraid and shame the most knowing Christian.[1]

In the *New Voyage Round the World*, which appeared in the following year, Defoe's narrator is less concerned with religion than Captain Johnson, but his remarks are also replete with praise for the virtues of the innocent savages. The natives encountered at Malacca have become accustomed to dealing with European traders. This contact with western civilization has made them 'fierce, cruel, treacherous, and merciless', while those who have encountered no Europeans at all are described in a passage which represents Defoe's closest approach to a glorification of the myth of the noble savage:

They went indeed naked, some of them stark naked, both men and women; but I thought they differed in their countenances from all the wild people that I ever saw; that they had something singularly honest and sincere in their faces; nor did we find anything of falsehood or treachery among them.[2]

The religion of these savages is closer to deism than to devil worship. Acting 'upon a more solid foundation, paying their reverence in manner much more rational, and to something which it was much more reasonable to worship', they prayed to the heavens and the stars.[3] Like Singleton, Defoe's narrator draws the conclusion that those savages who are corrupt have

[1] *A General History of the Robberies and Murders of the Most Notorious Pyrates* (1724-8), i. 199.
[2] Dent ed., xiv. 87, 117.   [3] Ibid., p. 148.

learned 'the treacherous and cruel part from others, which
nature gave them no ideas of before'.[1] It was a moral which
seems more appropriate to a follower of Shaftesbury than to a
champion of the English Dissenters.

With these examples in mind and with the realization that
Defoe's position on the subject of primitivism was becoming
increasingly paradoxical, the ideas contained in *Robert Drury's
Journal* should not seem at all extraordinary. Following the
suggestions made in various authentic accounts of the natives of
Madagascar, Defoe remarked that

... as the Natives have no Knowledge of the Curse on *Adam* and his
Posterity; so One would be tempted to think, as well for this Reason
as from their Colour, that they are not of his Race, or that the Curse
never reach'd them; for they can get their Living without the Sweat
of their Brows, or at least without that which we commonly understand by it; which is hard Labour.[2]

But although 'tempted' to think of Madagascar as a paradise,
Defoe quickly reverses this Utopian picture by showing how
human evil will destroy the abundance of nature by wars and
cruelty.

The moral of *Robert Drury's Journal* is not that man ought to
return to the purity of the state of nature but rather that even
in the midst of plenty the life of the savage is brutal and governed
by the passions. Although Defoe frequently idealized the savage
in order to satirize western society or as a fictional device, in the
majority of his writings he pictured the savage as an inferior
being, condemned to a bestial life on earth and to eternal tor-
ment after death. In the *Serious Reflections* Crusoe converses
with an old woman who tries to convince him that the cannibals
and all the other savages and barbarians whom he encountered
in his travels worshipped God. But Crusoe is not to be convinced. He advances the concept of the damnation of the
heathen, asserting that the devil rules all pagan nations, whose
worship is merely the product of fear.

[1] Dent ed., xiv, p. 176.   [2] *Madagascar*, p. 336.

Such an uncompromising attitude may appear surprising after an examination of Defoe's use of primitive ideas, but it was the most common concept of the savage in the seventeenth century. Any praise of the virtues of the primitive life was more than offset by the realistic accounts in Hakluyt's and Purchas's collections of voyages. Fontenelle's description of the American Indians as 'Animals of humane Shape, & that too sometimes very Imperfect, almost without humane Reason' was typical.[1] If the savages were not of the race of Adam, it was because, in the words of Richard Blackmore, they were 'a middle Species . . . a humane salvage Beast', a 'degenerate Race' abandoned by God.[2]

Because these accounts were so vivid, the *voyage imaginaire* seldom idealized the savage. Gabriel de Foigny, for instance, was careful to distinguish between his highly moral and deistical hermaphrodites and the natives of the Congo. He described the idleness of the Africans, not as a sign of their freedom from the curse of man's Fall, but as an indication of their addiction to the sin of sloth:

All these Considerations gave me an Idea of a People, who being not obliged to Labour, lived with some justice in the midst of Idleness, which rendered them dull, negligent, sleeping, disdainful, without Exercise, and without Action.[3]

The Utopias of Foigny, Vairasse, and Swift are inhabited by beings who are free from Adam's sin, but instead of ennobling the savages and placing them in this role, these authors peopled their imaginary lands with creatures whose creation was separate from the rest of mankind.

The Puritans' attitude towards the savages was even more severe than that of their contemporaries, and their attacks against the bestiality of the American Indian prompted Shaftesbury to

[1] Bernard de Fontenelle, *A Plurality of Worlds*, trans. John Glanvill (1929), p. 55.

[2] *The Nature of Man* (1711), pp. 22, 76.

[3] *A New Discovery of Terra Incognita Australis*, trans. John Dunton (1693), p. 22.

warn his readers against the captivity narratives which revealed
the savage as a mere animal impeding the progress of civilization. For Cotton Mather the Indian was a spawn of the Devil,
and where the colonists won a victory, there was God's triumph
over the soldiers of Satan. What the settlers expected to find
was a creature living under what Saint Paul called 'a law unto
themselves'. The Puritans believed that the Indian was a natural
man and that he could be expected to follow the laws of reason,
distinguish between good and evil, and worship some kind of
god. When, in 1622, the Indians revolted, the settlers felt that
the laws of nature had been violated.[1] Since the Indian did not
follow those rules written in his heart, he could no longer be
treated as a rational being. Hence Defoe's remarks on this Indian
war concern not only the treachery of the savages but also their
'folly'.[2]

Crusoe remarks that the cannibals sinned '. . . against that
Light which, as the Scripture says, was a Law to themselves,
and by such Rules as their Consciences would acknowledge to
be just, tho' the Foundation was not discover'd to us'.[3] What he
means is that the savages ought to be ruled by a law of reason
which is more explicit for them than for the Christian. Whereas
the Christian can rely on the less-demanding Covenant of
Grace, the savage is to be judged by the Covenant of Works.
By violating the laws of nature, the cannibals are sinning against
their conscience and against God. Their punishment will be
eternal damnation. If Crusoe feels that there is any injustice in
this, he also believes that man, who is 'Clay in the Hands of
the Potter', has no right to question God's will.[4]

In the *Serious Reflections* Crusoe maintains a paradoxical
defence of cannibalism, suggesting, as Montaigne had previously, that there was little difference between the warfare of
these anthropophagi and the contemporary European practice
of '. . . refusing quarter; for as to the difference between eating

---

[1] See Roy Harvey Pearce, *The Savages of America* (1953), p. 7.
[2] *Compleat English Tradesman*, i. 316.
[3] *Robinson Crusoe*, i. 244.   [4] Ibid., i. 244.

and killing those that offer to yield, it matters not much'.[1] But
this statement is located in the middle of a lengthy condemnation
of all pagan religions. The old gentlewoman maintains that since
the worship of God was a law of nature, it must be universal, but
Crusoe informs her that the universality of religious worship
was a myth, some savages having no religion at all. At best the
savage can succeed in attaining a natural religion, but without
revelation he is unable to apprehend Christianity. Friday is
unable to understand the existence of the Devil without a
thorough schooling from Crusoe, and the natives of Madagascar are merely amused by the story of the creation of Eve
from Adam's rib.[2] Only a Christian crusade, Crusoe maintains,
can save these people from damnation.

In his attack on the pagan world, Crusoe distinguishes between the savage and the barbarian. Garcilaso de la Vega had
argued that contrary to the cannibals of South America, the
Incas 'taught the natural laws to their people, and gave them
laws and precepts for a moral life.'[3] Defoe may have considered
this idea more dangerous than a glorification of the virtues of
the savage. As early as 1706 Defoe attacked the concept of the
sage Chinois in the *Consolidator*,[4] and Crusoe describes the
religion of the Chinese as 'nauseous and abominable', dismissing
entirely any claims made for the wisdom of Confucius.[5] Crusoe
even defends the cruelty of the Spaniards towards the natives
of Mexico and Peru:

We have heard much of the cruelty of the Spaniards in destroying
such multitudes of the inhabitants there, . . . but as I am for giving
up all the actions of men to the government of Providence, it seems to
me that Heaven had determined such an act of vengeance should
be executed, and of which the Spaniards were instruments, to

---

[1] p. 116.
[2] *Madagascar*, p. 187. See Thomas Burnet, *Archaeologiae Philosophicae*,
trans. Thomas Foxton (1729), pp. 18–21, 71, for the probable source of Defoe's
remarks on the Bible. See also *Jure Divino*, bk. iii, p. 9.
[3] *Royal Commentaries of the Yncas*, i. 101, 174.
[4] In *Early Life and Chief Earlier Works*, ed. Henry Morley (1889),
pp. 267–70.
[5] *Serious Reflections*, pp. 116–25.

destroy those people, who were come up (by the influence of the devil, no doubt) to such a dreadful height, in that abhorred custom of human sacrifices, that the innocent blood cried for it. . . .[1]

This passage contradicts Crusoe's attack on the cruelties of the Spaniards in the first volume and suggests that the closer Defoe's name became associated with *Robinson Crusoe* the more orthodox he became in religious matters.

The most bitter attacks on what might have been considered ideas favouring deism and primitivism occur in the *Serious Reflections*, where the distance separating Crusoe from Defoe has been erased by the author's contention that the work was allegorical. But it must be admitted that if the Crusoe who appears on the island is more tolerant than the Crusoe of the *Serious Reflections*, he is not substantially different. Crusoe's one moment of tenderness towards the cannibals amounts to his decision to abandon his senseless plan to slaughter great numbers of them in a sudden attack. This desire to kill them becomes an obsession with him, but he masters his passion for several reasons: he considers that they are innocent of any crime against him; that his action would be unnatural, since it would not be in self-defence; and what is clearly his main reason, that he is afraid that if any savages survived, they might kill him. Thus he acts mostly from 'Policy', restraining his disapproval of

. . . the unnatural Custom of that People of the Country, who it seems had been suffer'd by Providence in his wise Disposition of the World, to have no other Guide than that of their own abominable and vitiated Passions; and consequently were left, and perhaps had been so for some Ages, to act such horrid Things, and receive such dreadful Customs, as nothing but Nature entirely abandoned of Heaven, and acted by some hellish Degeneracy, could have run them into. . . .[2]

The key to the meaning of this passage lies in Defoe's use of the words 'unnatural' and 'nature'. It must be remembered that Defoe believed that 'all men are born knaves, villains, thieves, and murderers, and nothing but the restraining power of Pro-

---

[1] *Serious Reflections*, p. 214.   [2] *Robinson Crusoe*, i. 197.

vidence witholds us all from showing ourselves such on all occasions'.[1] These savages must be judged by a Covenant of Works, but like all men, they are ruled by their passions. When he calls the savages 'unnatural' Crusoe means that the law of nature which they have been granted has been entirely destroyed by their degenerate passions. The best thing Crusoe has to say of the cannibals is that they are as 'mild, and gentle' as most people in the world and 'as easily civilised'.[2]

For Defoe, nature led neither to the benefits of religion nor to the comforts of civilization. This is nowhere better illustrated than in Crusoe's attitude towards the nakedness of the savages. Although he seldom fails to remark on their lack of clothes, he refrains from comment until the *Serious Reflections*. In this last volume, however, Crusoe admits that the wearing of clothes is merely an effect of the Fall of Man 'and no virtue in itself, because no part of the body had been unfit to be exposed if vice had not made the distinction necessary'.[3] But to be ashamed of our nakedness is a sign of reason and the recognition of human sin. Crusoe calls for a truly innocent man, the noble, innocent savage, to present himself to the world: 'Let him come forth, let him go naked and live by himself, and let his posterity partake of his innocence'.[4] For such a man, nakedness would not be an evil, but he would have to live alone; he would have little resemblance to other human beings.

This invitation for such a man to appear is merely a rhetorical flourish, since no man on earth is free from the guilt of Adam, least of all the cannibals. Defoe was careful to describe Friday as an ideal specimen of cannibal manhood. His features are those of a European, and Crusoe frequently remarks on his athletic ability. But Friday's greatest virtue is his unquestioning acceptance of the values of civilization. Eager to imitate his master, Friday is happy to put on the clothes which Crusoe provides for him. Crusoe tells the reader, 'I . . . let him know, I would give him some Cloaths, at which he seem'd very glad,

[1] *Serious Reflections*, p. 23.   [2] Ibid., p. 116.
[3] Ibid., p. 93.   [4] Ibid., p. 94.

for he was stark naked'.[1] Of course, it is likely that Friday has never worn clothes in his life, but what greater indication of his awareness of sin than his eagerness to cover himself. This was no slip on Defoe's part. Crusoe's previous observations on nakedness are revealed as a prudish desire to clothe the natives, while Friday shows his intuitive knowledge of the laws of nature by his willingness to accept the token fig leaf which is offered to him.

But the significance of Friday's clothing is more than religious. It represents his first step towards civilization. Elsewhere Defoe remarked that it

... is to be said for the reputation of the Christian religion in general, and by which it is justly distinguished from all other religions, that wherever Christianity has been planted ... in the world, even where it has not had a saving influence, it has yet had a civilizing influence.[2]

Friday is distinguished not only by his readiness to accept Christianity but also by his willingness to accept the standards of western culture. Defoe praised the Portuguese for having 'so civilized the natives ... as to bring them, where they went even stark naked before, to clothe decently and modestly now'.[3] And Defoe rejoiced in the knowledge that these natives would never again return to that terrible state of nature which confused idleness and bestiality with happiness.

This attitude towards civilization and the state of nature was one which appears throughout the eighteenth century in writers whose interests, like Defoe's, were economic. Adam Smith, living in the second half of the century when the concept of the noble savage was a popular cliché, remarked that anyone who examined the culture of Mexico and Peru 'will evidently discern that, in arts, agriculture, and commerce, their inhabitants were much more ignorant than the Tartars of the Ukraine are at present'.[4] And Pufendorf believed that the sufferings of the

[1] *Robinson Crusoe*, i. 239.
[2] *Serious Reflections*, p. 112. See also *Plan of the English Commerce*, Shakespeare Head ed., p. 256.
[3] *An Humble Proposal*, Tegg ed., xviii. 28.
[4] *The Wealth of Nations* (1954), i. 185.

Aztecs and Incas under the Spaniards were entirely compensated for by the introduction of the European scissors and razor. Nowhere were Shaftesbury's ideas on natural virtue attacked so viciously as they were in the writings of Mandeville, for the doctrines of primitivism were anathema to an author who thought more in terms of material progress than human virtue. For Defoe and contemporary economists, the Hottentot, 'the worst and most savage of all Savages', wearing the entrails of his dead enemy, was the supreme example of the depths to which mankind could descend without the benefits of civilization.[1]

The pages of Hakluyt and Purchas provided ample evidence for the cultural backwardness of the savage. Martin Frobisher described the bestial life of the Indian in a passage with which Defoe was unquestionably familiar:

If they for necessities sake stand in need of the premisses, such grasse as the Countrey yeeldeth they plucke up and eate, not deintily, salletwise to allure their stomacks to appetite: but for necessities sake without either salt, oyles or washing, like brute beasts. . . . They neither use table, stoole, or table cloth for comlines: but when they are imbrued with blood knuckle deepe, and their knives in like sort, they use their tongues as apt instruments to lick them cleane.[2]

In several passages reminiscent of Frobisher's description, Crusoe contemplates what his life would have been like if he had not recovered his tools and weapons from the wreck. He thinks how, without a knife, he would have been forced to 'gnaw' at his prey with his teeth and pull at it with his hands 'like a meer Savage . . . like a Beast'.[3]

Crusoe's carpenter's chest is indeed 'more valuable than a Ship Loading of Gold'.[4] The Picart illustration, showing Crusoe with a saw, hatchet, and umbrella, which appeared in most continental editions of *Robinson Crusoe*, is far more significant

[1] *Atlas Maritimus & Commercialis* (1728), p. 237.
[2] Richard Hakluyt, *The Principle Navigations, Voyages, Traffiques and Discoveries of the English Nation* (1904), vii. 224.
[3] *Robinson Crusoe*, i. 150–1.   [4] Ibid., i. 57.

than the frontispiece in the original English edition which por-
trayed Crusoe with his muskets and sword. German and French
critics regarded *Robinson Crusoe* not as an adventure story but
as a parable of how an ordinary man might use his ingenuity to
reproduce the arts and inventions of civilization and by transforming his environment rescue himself from the state of nature.[1]

Crusoe is not exactly Prospero, for all his command over
nature, and Friday is far from a Caliban, but the gulf between
the civilized man and the savage is not easily bridged. For
Crusoe, Friday is never more than the best of servants; he is
not a friend. Although Crusoe regards the cannibals with a certain degree of tolerance, he never questions his superiority to
them and never abandons the values of his civilization. It is
Friday who learns to wear clothes, eat his food cooked, and
speak a new language. He even has to trade his God, Benamuckee, for Crusoe's. When Montaigne viewed some Indians
in Rouen, he was impressed with their innocence and intelligence; Defoe, viewing a similar spectacle, regarded the Indians
with contempt, remarking that having failed to benefit from
European civilization, they had decided to return to the 'Felicity
of Nakedness and Sloth in their own Country'.[2] No wonder
then that Friday, the ideal savage, should never question the
strange customs which Crusoe thrusts upon him.

IV

I was King and Lord of all this Country indefeasibly,
and had a Right of Possession; and if I could convey
it, I might have it in Inheritance, as compleatly as any
Lord of a Mannor in *England*.

> DEFOE, *The Life and Surprising Adventures of
> Robinson Crusoe*[3]

ROBINSON Crusoe survives his loneliness, conquers his environment and becomes the 'King' of his island, ruling, at first,

---

[1] See *La Vie et Les Avantures* (1720), p. viii; and Ludwig Vischer, trans.,
Das Leben und die ganze Ungemeine Vegebenheiten des Robinson Crusoe, 6th
ed. (1721), i. sigs. A2–A3.
[2] Lee, *Daniel Defoe*, ii. 182.   [3] i. 114.

over his parrot, goats, dog, and cat. Crusoe remarks, 'I was Lord of the whole Manor; or if I pleas'd, I might call my self King, or Emperor over the whole Country which I had Possession of. There were no Rivals.'[1] That Defoe was half-serious in suggesting Crusoe's right to call himself King of the island, there can be no doubt. Coleridge wondered whether Crusoe's claim was valid, but according to Grotius, islands in the sea belonged to the first inhabitant. Nor is there any doubt about the kind of monarch Crusoe is, for in the passage describing his 'Subjects', he reveals his absolute power: 'I had the Lives of all my Subjects at my absolute Command. I could hang, draw, give Liberty, and take it away, and no Rebels among all my Subjects.'[2] Concerning this speech, Rousseau remarked that Crusoe's despotic powers were indeed unlimited, but only so long as his subjects included no human beings. In spite of Rousseau's witty observation, Defoe seems to suggest that Crusoe's absolute control over the inhabitants of his island continues even after the arrival of human competitors. This presents a problem, for why should Defoe, an ardent opponent of tyranny, have made his hero into a despot. In order to understand Defoe's purpose, the *Surprising Adventures* and the *Farther Adventures of Robinson Crusoe* must be regarded as a single work concerned with the political evolution of society in the state of nature.

Defoe once advanced the argument that whoever owned the property of a nation was the actual ruler. He developed this idea by suggesting that foreigners might conquer England merely by buying up all the land, a theory which seemed absurd even to Walter Wilson, Defoe's most idolatrous biographer.[3] According to this dictum, Crusoe would have the same power as the Grand Seignior of the Turks whose ownership of the land gave him entire control over the lives and property of his people. But Crusoe establishes his absolutism on different ground. 'My people', he comments, 'were perfectly subjected: I was absolute

---

[1] *Robinson Crusoe*, i. 148.   [2] Ibid., i. 171.
[3] *The Original Power of the Collective Body of the People of England, Examined and Asserted* (1702 [1701]), pp. 18–20; and Walter Wilson, *Memoirs of the Life and Times of Daniel Defoe* (1830), i. 427.

Lord and Lawgiver; they all owed their Lives to me, and were ready to lay down their Lives, *if there had been Occasion of it*, for me.'[1] His claim to power is based on the right of conquest; every person who comes to the island is forced to swear complete obedience to his commands.

Crusoe's conquest of Friday follows the pattern of natural law which Grotius set forth in *De Jure Belli ac Pacis*.[2] Crusoe may be regarded as a monarch who is in a state of war with all those who threaten his kingdom. Friday is a prisoner of an enemy tribe which has a natural right to kill him, but Friday may legitimately attempt to preserve his life by escaping. Crusoe's slaughter of the cannibals pursuing Friday follows the natural laws of self-defence. By saving the life of Friday, who is also a cannibal and hence his enemy, Crusoe gains absolute dominion over him. At all times Crusoe has the right to kill Friday; instead he accepts a formal oath of complete obedience:

> When he espy'd me, he came running to me, laying himself down again upon the Ground, with all the possible Signs of an humble thankful Disposition, making a many antick Gestures to show it: At last he lays his Head flat upon the Ground, close to my Foot, and sets my other Foot upon his Head, as he had done before; and after this, made all the Signs to me of Subjection, Servitude, and Submission imaginable, to let me know, how he would serve me as long as he liv'd.[3]

Friday is Crusoe's slave because Crusoe has spared his life. Friday's father and the Spanish captain are also saved from the cannibals, and Crusoe accepts them as 'Subjects' who, like Friday, *'would die'* in Crusoe's defence.[4]

But Crusoe is less certain of the loyalty of the sixteen Spaniards and Portuguese whom he wants to bring over to his island. He tells the Spanish captain that since 'Gratitude was no inherent Virtue in the Nature of Man; nor did Men always square their Dealings by the Obligations they had receiv'd, so

---

[1] *Robinson Crusoe*, ii. 30.

[2] Trans. Francis Kelsey (1925), ii. 169–85 (II. i. 1–17); 641–657 (III. iv. 1–19).

[3] *Robinson Crusoe*, i. 239.   [4] Ibid., ii. 19.

much as they did by the Advantages they expected',[1] he is afraid that they might turn him over to the Inquisition if they reached Spanish territory. The Spanish captain assures the suspicious Crusoe that his fears are unjustified and promises that

· .. he would make Conditions with them upon their solemn Oath, That they should be absolutely under my Leading, as their Commander and Captain; and that they should swear upon the Holy Sacraments and the Gospel, to be true to me, and to go to such Christian Country, as that I should agree to, and no other; and to be directed wholly and absolutely by my Orders, 'till they were landed safely in such Country, as I intended; and that he would bring a Contract from them under their Hands for that Purpose.[2]

This contract is clearly different from the one which the Spanish captain swears he will follow:

Then he told me, he would first swear to me himself, That he would never stir from me as long as he liv'd, 'till I gave him Orders; and that he would take my Side to the last Drop of his Blood, if there should happen the least Breach of Faith among his Country-men.[3]

For Hobbes, gratitude was a law of nature which man ought to follow, but it did not always bind man 'in foro externo'.[4] Crusoe realizes this and, like a suspicious despot, he fears the rebellion of any of his subjects who have not sworn an oath of complete obedience.

Not satisfied with an oral oath, which Defoe regarded as entirely obligatory under the laws of nature, Crusoe insists on a written contract.[5] He tells the captain

... Not to bring any Man with him, who would not first swear. ... That he would no way injure, fight with, or attack the Person he should find in the Island, who was so kind as to send for them in order to their Deliverance; but that they would stand by and defend him against all such Attempts, and where-ever they went, would

[1] Ibid., ii. 34.   [2] Ibid., ii. 35.   [3] Ibid., ii. 35.
[4] *Leviathan*, p. 108. See also Howard Warrender, *The Political Philosophy of Hobbes* (1957), p. 67.
[5] See *The Wickedness of a Disregard to Oaths* (1723), pp. 8–14, 26–37. For Defoe's argument that a literal contract exists see *The Protestant Jesuite Unmask'd* (1704), p. 29.

be entirely under and subjected to his Commands; and that this should be put in Writing, and signed with their Hands.[1]

Defoe humorously has Crusoe admit that his insistence on a written contract might be difficult without pen, ink, or paper, but these obstacles do not deter his single-minded hero. Crusoe simply refuses to consider such technicalities.

He even asks for complete obedience from the Englishmen who are about to be marooned by their mutinous crew. The English captain makes an oral contract, swearing to 'be wholly Directed and Commanded' by Crusoe and promising that 'he would live and dye' at Crusoe's orders.[2] One might expect a generous disclaimer from Crusoe, for this is the first English-man he has seen for twenty-eight years. Instead he insists on passage to England and absolute obedience from them while they are on his island:

> That while you stay on this Island with me, you will not pretend to any Authority here; and if I put Arms into your Hands, you will upon all Occasions give them up to me, and do no Prejudice to me or mine, upon this Island, and in the mean time be govern'd by my Orders.[2]

There seems to be no question that Crusoe regards himself as a legally constituted monarch, jealous of his power and un-willing to allow anyone on the island who does not owe absolute obedience to him. Defoe seems to be saying that this kind of control over the lives of his subjects is the only kind of abso-lutism possible. It is significant that Crusoe has little influence upon the further development of the island, for his attitude towards the inhabitants is closer to that of a Louis XIV than to the patriarchal monarch he thinks he is.

Instead Defoe decided to depict the struggle of a society from the anarchy of the state of nature to an acceptance of law and limitations on freedom. With the coming of the Spaniards to the island there is merely a loose grouping of individuals: the three English mutineers led by Atkins, who is slothful but

---

[1] *Robinson Crusoe*, ii. 38.   [2] Ibid., ii. 47.

capable when he wishes to exert himself; the two diligent English sailors, who in spite of their efforts are not very fortunate; and the inhabitants of Crusoe's castle, including the Spanish captain, his sixteen followers, and Friday's father. They live in a state of nature without laws or any single authority; they have sufficient food, and there is no reason why they should not live together peacefully. But Atkins and his companions are ruled by their passions and refuse to live by the laws of nature and their touchstone: '*Do not that to another, which thou wouldest not have done to thy selfe.*'[1]

By their acts of violence against the other inhabitants of the island, they force the rest of the community to resort to the first law of nature, self-defence. The leader of the Spaniards, later made the Governor of Crusoe's colony, describes how it was necessary to create laws for their protection. 'I hope you will not be displeas'd', he remarks to Crusoe, 'when I shall tell you how forc'd by Necessity we were oblig'd, for our own Preservation, to disarm them. . . .'[2] The anarchy of the state of nature is always insufficient for constraining human evil. Will Atkins and his friends are like Hobbes's 'needy men and hardy, not contented with their present condition'.[3] The drive for power and the urgings of man's mischievous soul are too much for human nature where there are no laws to restrain the passions.

After the Spanish captain and his men arrive on the island, Atkins claims that he and his companions own the island and ought to be obeyed as absolute monarchs. This is the same claim which Crusoe makes to his island, but the Spanish Captain and the two diligent Englishmen know that the island belongs to Crusoe and reject Atkins's assertion of political and economic authority over them. The villains then decide to destroy the houses and farms of the two 'Honest' Englishmen, threatening the laws of property which exist in the state of nature, even though there is yet no legally constituted authority to protect possessions. The two wronged men appeal to the

---

[1] Hobbes, *Leviathan*, p. 108.
[2] *Robinson Crusoe*, ii. 148.　　　　　　　　[3] *Leviathan*, p. 63.

castle for help, and by force of numbers, they convince Atkins and his friends that they must make reparations for their crime. Although Atkins and his companions have violated the laws of nature which urge men to seek peace and to live justly, the Spanish captain, following these natural laws, refuses to pursue revenge and merely asks that they restore what they have destroyed. The punishment is significantly mild, for in the state of nature capital punishment may be inflicted only in the immediate defence of one's life.

Such violations of property indicated, according to Locke, a '. . . varying from the right rule of reason, whereby a man so far becomes degenerate, and declares himself to quit the principles of human nature and to be a noxious creature'.[1] Although Defoe clearly distinguished between a crime against property and a crime against human life, it is obvious from Atkins's behaviour that the social disorder of the state of nature is insufficient to cope with human evil. The laws of reason which direct man to seek happiness soon lead him to seek security and peace.

After a while, the crimes of Atkins and his men threaten the very lives of the rest of the colony. In a general meeting of the entire society, the Spanish captain tells the rebellious Englishmen that '. . . if they had been of his own Country, he would have hang'd them; for all Laws and all Governours were to preserve Society; and those who were dangerous to the Society, ought to be expell'd out of it'.[2] When it is discovered that Atkins planned to murder all the Spaniards while they slept, Atkins is banished from the castle. By forcing the three rebels to build their own homes and farm their own lands, the captain becomes the temporary magistrate and law-giver of the island, removing the society from the total anarchy of the state of nature. In *Jure Divino*, Defoe wrote:

> Society to Regulation tends,
> As naturally as Means pursue their Ends;

---

[1] *Two Treatises of Civil Government* (1955), p. 121.
[2] *Robinson Crusoe*, ii. 176.

The Wit of Man could never yet invent,
A Way of Life without a Government;
Subordination is the Soul of Law,
And Rules of Life to Rules of Living will draw;
What need had Power to prescribe the Man,
Let him go on without it if he can.[1]

The recalcitrants receive their banishment with a strange docility. Once law is established, it is usually obeyed. Swearing to obey the rules of the society, the English never again disturb the peace of the community.

The final solidification of the colony comes through 'Necessity' and the common need to preserve their lives as an army of cannibals descends upon the island to threaten the complete destruction of the community. Now the energies of Atkins and his two companions are directed towards a righteous war for self-defence. Defoe argued in *Jure Divino* that government was created from the necessity of a community to preserve its existence:

Necessity Confederate Heads Directs,
And Power United, Power Expos'd Protects;
The Nature of the Thing directs *the Mode*,
And Government was born in *Publick Good*:
Safety with *Right* and *Property* combines,
And thus *Necessity* with Nature *joins*.[2]

The conflict with the cannibals, therefore, strengthens what internal crime had already made necessary, and the inhabitants of Crusoe's island become members of a society with clearly defined laws of property and restraints on individual freedom.

There is a startling contrast between the brutality of the battle with the savages and Crusoe's attitude towards the cannibals. Indeed Crusoe's tolerance of primitive behaviour increases with age. In the *Farther Adventures* he enrages the crew of his nephew's ship by refusing to lend his approval to the '*Massacre of Madagascar*', his name for the crew's slaughter of an entire village in Madagascar. And when forced to kill some natives of Cochin-China in self-defence, Crusoe remarks:

[1] Bk. ii, p. 10.   [2] Bk. ii, p. 4.

I was sick of killing such poor Savage Wretches, even tho' it was in my own Defence, knowing they came on Errands which they thought just, and knew no better; and that tho' it may be a just Thing, because necessary, for there is no necessary Wickedness in Nature, yet I thought it was a sad Life, which we must be always oblig'd to be killing our Fellow-Creatures to preserve, and indeed I think so still.[1]

Crusoe's attitude reflects a Christian approach to the problem of self-defence and the laws of nature. He never denies a right of self-defence, but he seems to regret the fact that man cannot avoid his obligation to preserve his life.

The settlers on Crusoe's island reveal none of this reluctance. Acting in the name of 'Necessity', they slaughter their prisoners and, after the battle, hunt down the helpless survivors. Although the use of necessity as a justification for the colonists' actions in this conflict is kept within the rules of natural law in the conduct of warfare as laid down by Grotius, there is a clear reminder of Machiavelli's doctrine that men never do anything important 'unless necessity drives them to it'.[2] Defoe once confessed that necessity was 'the worst plea in the World, and generally made use of for the worst Things', yet he frequently resorted to the 'tyrant's plea', as Milton called it, to justify political and economic expediency.[3] The behaviour of the colonists may be closer to *raison d'état* than natural law, but unlike Crusoe they have been attacked by the cannibals and are too involved in their situation to speculate on the moral propriety of their actions.

After the skirmish with the cannibals, the colony adds thirty-seven of the remaining savages to their number, and many of them eventually become slaves and servants to the whites. In his study of the expansion of the colony through war and through the fertility of the five Englishmen who take native wives, Defoe

[1] *Robinson Crusoe*, iii. 129.
[2] Niccolò Machiavelli, *Discourses*, trans. Leslie Walker (1950), i. 217. See *A Collection of Miscellany Letters*, iii. 185 for Defoe's knowledge of the 'wise MACHIAVEL' and his doctrine of necessity.
[3] 'An Appeal to Honour and Justice' in *The Shortest Way with the Dissenters*, p. 225.

was obviously hinting at the same idea which Neville had exploited in his *Isle of Pines* and its sequel—the image of purity and vigour in a new land uncorrupted by the luxury of Europe. But unlike George Pine, Crusoe does not remain on the island to rule. He tells the reader:

I pleased my self with being the Patron of those People I placed there, and doing for them, in a kind of haughty majestick Way, like an old Patriarchal Monarch; providing for them, as if I had been Father of the whole Family, as well as of the Plantation: But I . . .left it as I found it, belonging to no Man; and the People under no Discipline or Government but my own; who, tho' I had Influence over them as Father and Benefactor, had no Authority or Power, to Act or Command one way or other, farther than voluntary Consent mov'd them to comply.[1]

Although Crusoe states that his colony has no government at all except a vague allegiance to him, it is actually a democracy. He compares himself to a 'Patriarchal Monarch', but except for sending a few supplies and some additional colonists, Crusoe does little to help the inhabitants of his island. Defoe once listed *'CAPACITY, INTEGRITY, COURAGE*, and *APPLICATION'* as the qualities of a good political leader.[2] Although Crusoe is certainly a capable man, his courage and integrity are questionable, and he certainly refuses to apply himself to the task of governing, preferring, instead, to travel around the world on a *'Wild Goose Chase'*.[3] In an attack upon the proprietary governors of the Carolinas, Defoe complained that

. . . they never learnt to be kings; . . . they have not taken the Hint of *Pater Patriae*, they don't know that a King must be the Father of his People; and that there is a sort of Patriarcal Affection, as well as Obligation, between a King on the Throne, and the People he Governs. . . .[4]

---

[1] *Robinson Crusoe*, iii. 80.
[2] *Rogues on Both Sides* (1711), p. 30.
[3] *Robinson Crusoe*, iii. 81.
[4] *Party-Tyranny*, p. 235. Although he wrote this pamphlet in 1705, Defoe's ideas on the government of the Carolinas were still vivid at the time he was writing the three parts of *Robinson Crusoe*. See, for example, *The Commentator* (11 April 1720).

Like the proprietors of Carolina, Crusoe bears little resemblance
to the patriarchal ruler, since he has little affection for his
people and no realization of the obligations which a monarch
must assume.

Crusoe is correct in stating that he left the island as he found
it but seems unaware that it is actually a democratic state just
barely removed from the state of nature. And this seems to
have been Defoe's concept of the ideal government. In spite of
some statements concerning a hero-king to whom all powers
might be surrendered, Defoe's Utopias always approach a type
of democracy which borders on anarchy. His attitude towards
revolution was more radical than Locke's, and he had none of
the conventional terror of mobs which appears in other Augustan
writers. Once he even defended the actions of some rioters, and
in his *Hymn to the Mob*, which purports to be an attack on
mob-rule, he wrote:

> Nor is thy Judgment *often wrong*,
> Thou seldom art mistaken, *never long;*
> However *wrong* in Means thou may'st appear,
> Thou gener'ly art in *thy Designs* sincere.[1]

Defoe regarded the 'Noun of Multitude' as the 'Original Power'
of government. In describing the democratic institutions of the
natives of Madagascar, he suggested that democracy was the
purest and most natural form of government:

. . . in the State of Nature, and the Beginning of Mens joining in
Societies, this was the Form of Government; and with due Reverence to the Learned, I think, we need not turn over many Volumes
to find the Original of *British Parliaments*; for they are earlier than
all their Histories, or even Letters themselves; and as to their Power,
it is founded on the strongest *Basis*, REASON and NATURE.[2]

But the democracy of these natives is not merely a savage form
of government. Defoe's hero, Captain Misson, the captain of
the pirate ship, *Victoire*, and ruler of the Utopian colony,

---

[1] p. 11. See his letter to Harley in which he argues that 'Generally
Speaking the Common People have been Allwayes in the Right.' *The Letters
of Daniel Defoe*, ed. George Healey (1955), p. 33.
[2] *Madagascar*, p. 155.

Libertalia, refuses to use his powers of command, depending instead upon the will of the majority among his followers. Even after a more stable government is established at Libertalia, the form is entirely democratic. Misson is elected for a three-year term as 'Conservator' and rules with the assistance of a parliament.[1]

Although Defoe apparently thought that democracy was the ideal form of government, he may have regarded it as impractical. Misson's colony is destroyed through its very basic belief in human equality, while the inhabitants of Crusoe's island have already begun to depart from economic equality. In any society, natural talents and diligence separate the superior man from the slothful—the master from the servant. Crusoe's colony languishes because Crusoe fails to help the inhabitants, but it becomes clear that had the community survived, it would eventually have been like any other West-Indian settlement. Observing the effects of the labour of the two industrious Englishmen in contrast to the farms of Atkins and his friend, Crusoe reads the moral: 'The Diligent liv'd well and comfortably, and the Slothful liv'd hard and beggarly; and so I believe, generally speaking, it is all over the World'.[2]

Crusoe's colony fails when left to its own resources, but this does not mean that Crusoe could have ruled the island as an absolute monarch had he remained. Defoe once remarked that the power of the patriarch depended upon kindness, wisdom, and the authority of age. Where the father was cruel the son could not be expected to obey.[3] Crusoe's original claims to power, the right of conquest, possession, and a contract of absolute obedience, would hardly have stood the test of time. When he gives away his land upon vague and generous terms of rental, he is merely ratifying the colonists' right to keep what they have already possessed through their labour. Thus Crusoe's concept of himself as a monarch, whether absolute or patriarchal,

---

[1] *General History of the Pyrates*, ii. 14, 99–101.
[2] *Robinson Crusoe*, ii. 193.
[3] *Jure Divino*, bk. ii, p. 2.

is a delusion; his surrender of command over the inhabitants of the island is little more than a histrionic gesture.

Crusoe's island therefore reveals the development of society, but Defoe was unable to present this idea without removing his hero from the scene. Crusoe was useful for presenting the solitary man in the state of nature, but he was an obstacle in the way of Defoe's attempt to present his theories on the political evolution of society. For Defoe had a specific example in mind— the early history of Bermuda. It has often been suggested that certain similarities exist between Shakespeare's *Tempest* and *Robinson Crusoe*, but while Defoe probably knew the play in its original form or in Dryden's adaptation, he was unquestionably familiar with Shakespeare's sources as well as numerous other accounts of the history of Bermuda.[1]

The first person to land on Bermuda, Henry May, resembles Crusoe only to the extent that he rescued his carpenter's tools from his ship and used his ingenuity to construct another vessel by which he escaped. But the arrival of Somers and his men resulted in the same kind of disputes which plagued the island after Crusoe's departure. One of the crew, Stephen Hopkins, contended that all governmental authority had been dissolved by the wreck and that it was

. . . no breach of honesty, conscience, nor Religion to decline from the obedience of the Governour, or refuse to goe any further, led by his authority (except it so pleased themselves) since the authority ceased when the wracke was committed, and with it, they were all freed from the government of any man.[2]

After frequent quarrels three men were left on the island in the manner of Atkins and his two companions. In almost every account these three were described as kings or rulers of the

---

[1] See, for example, John Robert Moore, 'The Tempest and Robinson Crusoe', *RES*, xxi (January 1945), 52–56; and 'The Canon of Defoe's Writings', *Library*, xi (September 1956), 167–9. Defoe refers to the history of Bermuda in *Jure Divino*, bk. viii, p. 12; in *A General History of Trade*, No. 1 (July 1713), p. 40; and in *Atlas Maritimus & Commercialis* (1728), pp. 307–9. The latter is a lengthy retelling of the story to illustrate the 'Nature of Man'. See also *Review*, iii. 518.

[2] Samuel Purchas, *Hackluytus Posthumus* (1907), xix. 30.

island. Oldmixon remarked that they 'were sole Lords of the Country, but like Kings of the World they soon fell out among themselves'.[1]

In retelling this story in his *Atlas Maritimus & Commercialis*, Defoe used the quarrels of these 'Lords of the Island' as an example of 'the contentious quarrelsome Nature of Man, and how impossible it is for him to agree with his fellow Creatures, if the least View of Profit or Glory comes in the way'.[2] This moral constitutes Defoe's primary indebtedness to the history of Bermuda for the *Farther Adventures*, although there are numerous parallel incidents.[3] The extent of Defoe's borrowings, however, is less significant than the enormous changes he made. Here, as with the story of Selkirk in the *Life and Surprising Adventures*, Defoe was mainly concerned with the central concept. He was not trying to fictionalize the story of Bermuda's first colonists, but to show how laws arose in the state of nature both because and in spite of the 'Nature of Man' and how the existence of property and certain restraints upon freedom preceded the creation of a strongly centralized state.

Rousseau wrote that 'when we leave the state of nature we compel others to do the same; no one can remain in a state of nature in spite of his fellow-creatures'.[4] This remark concerns Émile, whom Rousseau described as a natural man living in civilization, but it also suggests the lesson of Crusoe's island. Crusoe is committed to living a life which is as close to civilized existence as the limitations of his mind and body and the resources of the island will permit. He departs from the solitary state of nature with the arrival of Friday and then proceeds to educate his servant in order to remove Friday from the state of

[1] John Oldmixon, *The British Empire in America* (1741), ii. 442.
[2] p. 308. See also *Jure Divino*, bk. vii, p. 12.
[3] Besides the obvious resemblance between Atkins and his gang and Chard, Carter, and Waters, there is also a concern with hunger and isolation, discovering treasure, shipwrecks, and even some plants which spring up miraculously. See John Smith, *The General Historie of the Bermudas, Works*, ed. Edward Arber (1884), pp. 41, 638–40, 645, 652, 656; and *The Historye of the Bermudaes*, ed. J. Henry Lefroy (1882), pp. 41, 63–68.
[4] *Emile*, trans. Barbara Foxley (1911), p. 156.

nature in regard to Christianity, civilized behaviour, and the manufacturing and agricultural crafts. After Crusoe and Friday leave the island, the colonists live in a political state of nature, until the Spanish captain forces everyone to recognize the sanctity of property and restrictions on individual freedom; until, in other words, the establishment of law removes the society from the state of nature. Although Crusoe is occasionally content with his isolation, Friday with his religion and savage customs, and the islanders probably happy enough to be living without the restrictions of government, it is obvious that the state of nature is not the best of human conditions. Without social intercourse, civilization, and government, mankind cannot for long live comfortably, securely, or happily.

III

THE PROBLEM OF NECESSITY IN
DEFOE'S FICTION

I

I tell you, Sir, you would not Eat your Neighbours Bread
only, but your Neighbour himself, rather than Starve,
and your Honesty would all Shipwrack in the Storm of
Necessity.

DEFOE, *A Review of the Affairs of France*[1]

IN the second section of the *Serious Reflections of Robinson
Crusoe*, Defoe's aged hero indulges in a philosophical essay on
the 'Trial of Honesty'. 'Necessity', Crusoe begins, 'makes an
honest man a knave; and if the world was to be the judge
according to the common received notion, there would not be
an honest poor man left alive.'[2] Although this discourse throws
almost no light on Crusoe's character, it contains Defoe's most
thorough treatment of dishonesty and guilt, a central problem
in his fiction. When Moll Flanders, Colonel Jack, and Roxana
attempt to excuse their crimes, they plead their 'Necessity'.
Such a plea is meaningless when judged by the 'common received notion' of morality or by the English common law, but
has a significant place in contemporary discussions of natural
law. Before the guilt or innocence of Defoe's characters can be
determined, they must be judged at what Defoe once called the
'Bar of Nature'.[3]

'The *Case* of Necessity', wrote Samuel Pufendorf, 'is a thing
in every Body's Mouth, and the force of it generally acknow-
ledg'd in the World: Hence we commonly say, that it *hath no*

---

[1] iii. 109*b*.   [2] p. 33.
[3] *Memoirs of the Conduct of Her Late Majesty and Her Last Ministry*
(1715), p. 4.

Law, that 'tis a *suppos'd* or *presumptive* Exception to all Human
Ordinances and Constitutions; and that therefore it gives a
Right of doing many things, otherwise forbidden.'[1] For Defoe
and his contemporaries, 'Necessity' indicated a state of desperation, usually associated with starvation and destitution, in which
the victim is forced to choose between certain death or a life
prolonged only by violating the laws of society, religion, or
personal honour. In debating the problems of necessity most
writers chose sides according to their attitude towards self-
preservation. If they believed that self-preservation was the
primary and unalterable law of nature, they usually contended
that man could not resist temptation when he was starving.
Defoe always took this stand, maintaining that man did not
surrender the right of self-preservation when he left the state
of nature in order to enter society. As we have seen, throughout
his writings self-defence is an instinctual and obligatory act:

> No Man was ever yet so void of Sense,
> As to debate the Right of Self-Defence,
> A Principle so grafted in the Mind,
> With Nature born, and does like Nature bind:
> Twisted with Reason, and with Nature too;
> As neither one nor t'other can undo.[2]

It is hardly surprising that, holding these views, Defoe should
have sympathized with '. . . honest Men made Knaves by in-
supportable Necessity'.[3]

In one of the most characteristic passages on this subject in
the *Review*, Defoe attacked the idea of a rigid principle of
honesty as totally incompatible with the realities of human
nature:

> I am of the Opinion that we have generally Mistaken Notions
> in the World, about Honesty, and those that have never had occa-
> sion to try their Integrity, are too apt to censure those that have;
> I believe there are Occasions, in which the Necessity is too hard,

---

[1] *Law of Nature*, p. 156 (II. vi. 1).
[2] 'The True Born Englishman', in *The Shortest Way with the Dissenters*,
p. 58.
[3] Lee, *Defoe*, iii. 17.

even for Humane Nature it self, tho' backed with Reason, and Fortify'd with Religion; how else have we known Men driven to the Necessity of Eating one another, and very Solemnly say Grace, or Crave a Blessing upon the Horrid Repast? Were the Honestest Man in the World, Brought to the Necessity of Starving, he would not only borrow when he could not Pay, but Steal or do any thing. . . . I firmly believe, there never was a Man so Honest, but would *Steal*, before he would *Starve*, and if he did not, it was want of Opportunity.[1]

Not only is Defoe's position extreme, but it places him in company with such suspect thinkers as Hobbes, Spinoza, and Mandeville. On the other side, following the tradition of Cicero, were the more conventional moralists. In his germinal discussion of necessity, Cicero had argued that 'the greatest necessity is that of doing what is honourable (*honestatis*)' and that man should value virtuous actions above his life.[2] Among the adherents of this point of view were almost all the opponents of Hobbes: Clarendon, Eachard, J. Shafte, Cumberland, Lowde, Tyrrel, and Locke. Lowde's argument that martyrs do not suffer pain for surrendering 'the short and transitory satisfaction of a frail Life' was perhaps the most emphatic in its denial of a strong principle of self-preservation.[3] By the eighteenth century, writers such as Shaftesbury, Hutcheson, and Wollaston were contending that virtue and truth were far more important to man than his desire to preserve his life.[4]

Although most English philosophers came to reject necessity and self-preservation as excuses for stepping outside the boundaries of morality, necessity remained an important problem through the influence of Grotius and Pufendorf, the two great commentators on natural law. John Locke, who refused to inflict too much learning on his ideally educated gentleman, did

---

[1] iii. 109*a*.
[2] *De Inventione*, trans. H. M. Hubbel (1949), p. 341.
[3] James A. Lowde, *A Discourse Concerning the Nature of Man* (1694), pp. 174–80.
[4] See especially Wollaston, *The Religion of Nature Delineated*, p. 20. Cf. John Clarke, *An Examination of the Notion of Moral Goodness and Evil* (1725), pp. 12–34.

not hesitate to recommend Pufendorf's *De Jure Naturae et Gentium* and Grotius's *De Jure Belli ac Pacis* as works on a subject 'which a gentleman should not barely touch at, but constantly dwell upon, and never have done with'.[1] Some indication of the thoroughness of these treatises may be found in Josiah Fribble's letter to the *Spectator* inquiring if either Grotius or Pufendorf had made any comments on '*Pin-money*'.[2] By searching through the indexes of their writings, the reader might discover almost every legal, economic, political, and ethical problem thoroughly discussed and solved according to the rules of reason and nature. For so prolific a journalist and pamphleteer as Defoe such works were of enormous value. It is not surprising, therefore, to find references to both Grotius and Pufendorf in Defoe's writings and more than ten volumes of their works listed in the catalogue of his library.[3]

Although Grotius's reasoning on necessity followed naturally from his ideas on self-preservation, he did not simply argue that natural law allowed each man the right to defend his life. Like Aquinas, Grotius contended that necessity returned society to a state of nature in which all property was held in common. An individual who was starving could take whatever was available to assuage his hunger because when he was in this condition he had a right to the food as a member of the community.[4] At times Defoe seems to have accepted this explanation. 'Distress', he once wrote, 'removes from the Soul, all R[e]lation, Affection,

---

[1] 'Some Thoughts Concerning Education', in *On Politics and Education*, ed. Howard Penniman (1947), p. 362.

[2] Joseph Addison, *The Spectator*, No. 295.

[3] Professor John Robert Moore has kindly called my attention to these items and to several passages in which Defoe mentions Grotius and Pufendorf. See *Librorum ex Bibliothecis Philippi Farewell, D.D., et Danielis DeFoe* (1731), items 90, 127, 190, 289, 609, 691, 694, 831, 845, 848. Although Farewell may have owned some of these books, Defoe's knowledge of law was extensive. See, for example, *The Unreasonableness and Ill Consequences of Imprisoning the Body for Debt* (1729), pp. 8–25. Defoe cites both Grotius and Pufendorf in *Jure Divino*, bk. i, p. 19; and bk. iii, p. 25. Defoe's remark that he had 'a very great Veneration' for Grotius is higher praise than he ever gave Locke or Sidney. See *A Speech without Doors* (1710), p. 6.

[4] Grotius, *De Jure Belli ac Pacis*, ii. 193 (II. ii. 6). See also Thomas Aquinas, *Summa Theologica*, II. II. lxvi. 7 and II. II. xxxii. 7.

Sense of Justice, and all the Obligations, either Moral or Religious, that secure one Man against another.'[1] But while suggesting a dissolution of the society into the state of nature, Defoe never commented on a change in the status of property. There are good reasons for this. As we have seen, Defoe argued for the existence of private property in the state of nature, and for all his inconsistencies, he never revealed any leaning towards the ideas of the Levellers.

On this point, Defoe's position was closer to that of Pufendorf, who also found Grotius's argument unacceptable. Pufendorf remarked that if necessity does actually return the thief to a state in which there is no ownership of goods, then there can be no problem of guilt. If there is no guilt involved in theft, there is no need for the restitution of property upon which Grotius insisted. As a solution to this dilemma, Pufendorf substituted a concept of imperfect right governed by the conditions which brought the thief into his necessity.[2] In the same manner, Defoe warned his readers that they should not mistake his meaning, for necessity does not remove guilt: '*No, no, Gentlemen*, you will see the Crime lyes deeper than the Fact; Necessity will make us all Thieves, *but the Crime is in the Cause of that Necessity*; and he that will impartially examine his Circumstances, and place things in a True Light, will see, that the *Methods to bring him into that Necessity*, Govern the Case.'[3] Defoe believed that there were three possible ways to fall into necessity: through vice and intemperance; through want of judgement; and through insufficient knowledge or reason, as in the case of idiots or minors. He is willing to excuse both natural ignorance and inexperience, but vice is never a sufficient plea.[4]

Although Defoe frequently referred to natural law and necessity throughout his writings, his most systematic discussion appeared in the *Serious Reflections of Robinson Crusoe*. Here, in his example of the starving shipwrecked sailors drawing lots to determine who will offer himself as the next meal; in

---

[1] *Review*, viii. 302*b*.   [2] *Law of Nature*, pp. 161–2 (II. vi. 5–6).
[3] *Review*, iii. 113*a*.   [4] *Serious Reflections*, p. 44.

insisting that any harmful act committed against persons in similar necessity, e.g. a thief who robs someone as destitute as himself, was a violation of the law of nature; and in suggesting that
restitution should be made whenever possible, Defoe followed
closely the patterns of argument and some of the examples used
by Grotius and Pufendorf. But he disagreed with both of them
on a few essential points of doctrine. While agreeing that it was
wrong for a necessitous person to harm an individual in a
similar state of necessity, Defoe did not believe that anyone
could resist using all his efforts to save his own life. In spite of
the importance which Grotius gave to the idea of self-preservation in his system of natural law, Grotius referred approvingly
to Lactantius's opinion that a man would rather drown than
attempt to wrest from its possessor a plank which could only
support one person.[1] In contrast, Defoe agreed with the Hobbist
of antiquity, Carneades, in maintaining that no moral con-
sideration would prevent a man from doing his utmost to
survive:

> Will the honestest Man of you all, if ye were drowning in the
> *Thames*, refuse to lay hold of your Neighbour who is in the same
> Condition, for fear he drown with you? Nay, will you not pull him
> down by the Hair of his Head, tread on him with your Feet, tho'
> you sink him to the Bottom, to get your self out?[2]

Defoe was unable to believe that moral principle or even
Christian virtue was strong enough to overrule the law of self-
preservation. 'Necessity', he argued, 'is above the power of
human nature, and for Providence to suffer a man to fall into
that necessity is to suffer him to sin, because nature is not
furnished with power to defend itself, nor is grace itself able to
fortify the mind against it.'[3]

Defoe's most vivid picture of what he called the 'extremes
of necessity' occurs in the *Farther Adventures*. Crusoe's ship
encounters a vessel which has been damaged by a storm. Low

---

[1] Grotius, *De Jure Belli ac Pacis*, ii. 194 (II. ii. 8). See also Lactantius,
Works, trans. William Fletcher, in *Ante Nicene Christian Library* (1871),
xxi. 322.
[2] *Review*, viii. 302*b*.   [3] *Serious Reflections*, p. 34.

on food for days, the starving crew has refused to provide any
food for the passengers. Crusoe describes how impossible it is
to keep the crew from devouring the food too quickly for their
weakened condition, since 'Words are indeed of very small Force
to an hungry Belly'.[1] The passengers, including a woman, her
seventeen-year-old son, and a maid, are almost dead, and indeed
the woman dies soon after Crusoe and his men board the ship.
Crusoe observes that it is actually a case of murder, but he
excuses the crew because 'Hunger knows no Friend, no Relation, no Justice, no Right, and therefore is remorseless, and
capable of no Compassion'.[2] Nor did Defoe ignore his opportunity to exploit a subject which apparently fascinated him.
Asked by Crusoe to describe the sensations of hunger, the maid
details her pains and delusions. She tells how in her torments
she was tempted to bite her own arm and how after a nose bleed
she eagerly drank her own blood. She affirms that had she been
a mother she might have eaten her own child in her delirium and
confesses that as much as she loved her mistress she would have
eaten her with 'Relish'.[3]

Crusoe also suggests that the crew would soon have been
forced to eat one another in order to survive. Pufendorf wrote
that to 'feed on Man's Flesh in the desperate Extremity of
Famine, when no other Sustenance can be procur'd, is a lament-
able indeed, but not a sinful Expedient'.[4] And, commenting on
a famous case, he argued that the seven Englishmen who were
forced to murder one of their group in order to save themselves
from starvation were innocent. Defoe agreed with this decision,
but whereas Pufendorf justified the sailors on the grounds that
the man who was killed died with less grief to himself than to his
companions, Defoe merely appealed to 'necessity to palliate the
crime', and refusing to offer any moral justification for the
murder, concluded that 'necessity makes the highest crimes
lawful, and things evil in their own nature are made practicable

---

[1] *Robinson Crusoe*, ii. 139. Cf. Pufendorf, *Law of Nature*, p. 158 (II. vi. 3):
'the Belly that Advocate without Ears'.
[2] *Robinson Crusoe*, ii. 142.   [3] Ibid., iii. 67.
[4] Pufendorf, *Law of Nature*, p. 158 (II. vi. 3).

by it'.[1] Thus although he spared the reader the details of cannibalism among civilized men, Defoe's description of the hunger of the maid leaves no doubt that he regarded necessity as a force above all human morality or virtue.

Defoe also differed from most philosophers of natural law in his failure to distinguish between poverty and necessity. The Biblical text which he quotes is Proverbs xxx. 7, 'Give me not Poverty lest I steal', but in its context this is merely a plea for a middle state between poverty and wealth. In trying to persuade his son to seek neither poverty nor riches, Robinson Crusoe's father used this quotation in its customary sense.[2] If Defoe has little authority from the philosophers for this radical departure, he has even less from the religious treatises of his fellow Dissenters. Matthew Henry in his exhaustive commentary on the Bible published in 1710 stated that the example of David's eating the shewbread (Matthew xii. 1–4) may give some justification for theft in dire necessity, but on the text which Defoe usually cites, he commented, 'It will not bear them out at God's bar, no more than at men's.'[3] And Richard Baxter in his *Christian Directory* refused to admit necessity as a justification for violating the property of others. 'A dear price', he exclaimed, 'to buy the food that perisheth, with the loss and hazard of everlasting life.'[4]

Does this mean that Defoe's ideas were entirely outside the pale of Puritan thought? An answer to this question may be found in William Ames's *Conscience*, a monument of Puritan piety and perhaps one of Defoe's school-books.[5] Ames argued that the victim of the thief should not be angry provided that the thief stole

---

[1] *Serious Reflections*, pp. 35–36.   [2] *Robinson Crusoe*, i. 3.
[3] *An Exposition of the New and Old Testament*, 4th ed. (1737), ii, sig. 18 O_2. Defoe occasionally used Matthew xxi. 4, as well as Proverbs vi. 30, 'Men do not despise a thief, if he steal to satisfy his soul when he is hungry', but these are useless when he is trying to identify the laws of necessity with poverty. See *Serious Reflections*, p. 40; and Lee, iii. 16.
[4] *Practical Works* (1707), i. 490.
[5] See Lew Girdler, 'Defoe's Education at Newington Green Academy', *SP*, l (October 1953), 583.

. . . to succour his owne present extreame necessity, which hee could not helpe by any other meanes. For this seems to be the law of nature more ancient than the division of things, which cannot be abrogated by humane law, by which the division of things was made: In which sense it is not ill said, that all things are made common in urgent necessity.[1]

While admitting that there are degrees of necessity, Ames made no effort to distinguish between extreme want and simple poverty in relation to the degrees of guilt involved in any criminal act. Thus Ames, like Defoe, saw little difference between the necessitous thief and the destitute beggar, both having the same claim upon human charity. Although Ames's comments on necessity are brief, they may well have had a formative influence on Defoe's thought.

II

> I am perswaded, no Man ever takes the High-way, but from the Case of the Unjust Steward; *Dig I cannot, and to Beg I am asham'd: What shall I do?* An *English* Gentleman would presently have said to himself, Do! What should you do? Get a Horse, and a Case of Pistols; Is not the Highway wide enough?
>
> DEFOE, *A Review of the Affairs of France*[2]

As might be expected, Defoe's ideas on necessity found their fullest realization in his fiction. Not only did he utilize the basic situation of a character or group of characters forced to commit crimes because of their poverty, but he also adapted necessity–crime–restitution as the pattern for most of his social fiction. Unfortunately we cannot always accept the plea of necessity as an indication of the innocence of Defoe's heroes and heroines. When he writes of the temptations of necessity in his *Review* or in pamphlets attacking the evils of the bankruptcy and debtors' laws, we know that Defoe is pleading his own case, that he is thinking of his own struggles with his creditors and his business failures.[3] We can even accept Robinson Crusoe's disinterested

[1] v. i. 1.   [2] i. 350.
[3] See, for example, Defoe, *Remarks on the Bill to Prevent Frauds Committed by Bankrupts* (1706), pp. 5–23.

comments on necessity as an indication of Defoe's true feelings. But when, in *The Four Years Voyages of Capt. George Roberts*, the pirate Russel argues succinctly that '*Self-Preservation is the first Law of Nature, and Necessity, according to the old Proverb, has no Law*',[1] we know that the speaker is a complete villain and that he is by no means in a state of necessity. Confronted with a similarly doubtful plea by the grave-diggers in *A Journal of the Plague Year*, Defoe's narrator remarks, 'It is true, Necessity was a very justifiable warrantable Plea, and nothing could be better; but their Way of Talk was much the same, where the Necessities were not the same'.[2] Thus before we can acquit Defoe's characters at the 'Bar of Nature', we must determine the reality, degree, and cause of their necessity.

The most obvious example of Defoe's fictional treatment of this problem is in *The History of Colonel Jack*, where crime is entirely excused on the plea of necessity caused by youth and innocence. In his preface Defoe states that '*Circumstances form'd him by Necessity to be a Thief*', utilizing the word 'necessity' in the dual sense of poverty and causation.[3] But not satisfied with this plea, Defoe insists on Jack's *naïveté* and childishness. We are told over and over again that he is entirely ignorant of money and all the affairs of life. 'I knew no Good and had tasted no Evil', Jack says of himself after his childhood crimes, and he pointedly refers to his condition as a 'State of Ignorance'.[4] Describing himself as 'a poor Innocent Boy', Jack excuses his youth with the comment that he 'set out into the World so early, that when he began to do Evil, he understood nothing of the Wickedness of it, nor what he had to expect for it'.[5] And like Crusoe's savages, Jack is shown as innocent of any sin against his conscience:

NOTHING is more certain than that hitherto being partly from the gross ignorance of my untaught Childhood, as I observ'd before,

---

[1] (1726), p. 56.
[2] Shakespeare Head ed., p. 256.
[3] *The History of Colonel Jack*, Shakespeare Head ed., i. vii.
[4] Ibid., i. 47. The word 'Ignorance' appears incorrectly as 'Innocence' in this edition.   [5] Ibid., i. 5.

partly from the Hardness and Wickedness of the Company I kept, and add to these, that it was the Business I might be said to be brought up to, I had, *I say*, all the way hitherto, no Manner of Thoughts about the Good or Evil of what I was embark'd in; consequently, I had no Sense of Conscience, no Reproaches upon my Mind for having done amiss.[1]

In order to justify his plea Defoe was not only placing Jack in the category of the irrational but also insisting on his hero's condition as reflecting a state of nature. Both of these ideas were entirely conventional. Eachard remarked in his attack upon Hobbes that everyone knew children to be 'in the true state of nature', and all the writers on natural law agreed that no one could be held responsible for having violated a law which was above his capacity to understand.[2]

Although in his narration Jack refers to his condition as 'Necessity', he is never actually starving.[3] During his childhood he has no insight into any moral problems involved in his life of crime. Merely a child following natural laws to preserve his life, Jack has no intention of harming others, and he is scrupulous about returning all personal notes which are of no use to him. Colonel Jack is Defoe's Emile, the natural man living in society. He follows the laws of nature which dictate self-interest and takes from society only what he needs to stay alive.

The act which removes him from the state of nature is, significantly enough, the one act which a person in a state of necessity is not allowed to commit without sinning against the law of nature—theft from a person in a similar condition. Grotius argued that 'if the owner himself is under an equal necessity . . . the position of the owner gives him the preference'.[4] Although Defoe argued that no man could refrain from taking that which would preserve his life, Jack is already beyond the poverty of his childhood when he robs a poor old woman. He

---

[1] Ibid., i. 70.
[2] John Eachard, *Mr. Hobb's State of Nature Considered* (1672), pp. 69–71.
[3] *Colonel Jack*, i. 124.
[4] *De Jure Belli ac Pacis*, ii. 194 (II. ii. 8).

never steals afterwards, for this is his introduction to the real world and to maturity. His age (eighteen) has taken from him the excuse of irrationality, and his increased wealth has removed him from poverty. It is his last crime before leaving London to seek his fortune. But before he goes, Jack insists on returning the money which he had stolen from the old woman. As we have seen, Defoe counselled restitution after the dangers of necessity were passed, and Jack feels it his duty to right the wrong he has committed. After receiving both the forgiveness and thanks of the wronged woman, Jack wonders whether he ought to make restitution to all his victims but soon dismisses the idea as impracticable. It is questionable whether any of his former thefts were real crimes since they were committed in accordance with the laws of nature, and then, to return all the money would restore Jack to the same state of necessity as before. Like Captain Singleton, Jack retains the money that he has stolen, although unlike Defoe's more acquisitive hero, he never promises to tell how he preserved a 'ruined Family' whom he had plundered.[1]

Colonel Jack provides the best example of the cycle of necessity in Defoe's fiction. Born into poverty and hunger, the hero is forced by the laws of nature to violate the positive laws of his country, but when he commits a crime against the laws of nature, he makes restitution. Jack falls into poverty once more when he goes to Scotland, but he refuses to steal, preferring to join the army in order to avoid starvation. 'I had a secret Satisfaction at being now under no Necessity of stealing . . .', he remarks, and he even prefers the arduous servitude in Virginia to the horror of his former life:

. . . how Happy I was, that I cou'd live by my own Endeavours, and was no more under the Necessity of being a Villain, and of getting my Bread at my own Hazard, and the ruin of honest Families; this had in it something more than commonly pleasing and agreeable, and in particular, it had a Pleasure, that till then I had known nothing

[1] *Colonel Jack*, i. 103. Cf. *Captain Singleton*, p. 327; and *Street-Robberies, Consider'd* (1728), p. 48.

of: It was a sad Thing to be under a Necessity of doing Evil, to procure that Subsistence, which I could not support the want of, to be oblig'd to run the Venture of the Gallows, rather than the Venture of Starving, and to be always wicked for fear of Want.[1]

It is interesting to observe that Jack equates Necessity with a 'fear' of starving rather than the actual physical sensation, with poverty rather than hunger. As for his sadness at committing evil, it is like Crusoe's dejection at killing to stay alive, a reflection which says more about the character of the speaker than his beliefs.

An even broader definition of necessity appears in the narrative of Jack's tutor and manager. This transported felon has none of Jack's excuses, having fallen into necessity through 'a loose life'. Thus, in spite of the sympathy with which Defoe pleads his cause, the tutor's situation fits into a category which is not truly excused by a plea of necessity. His education is an especially important point against him, since he cannot plead ignorance. But the tutor makes a case for the irresistible power of necessity:

. . . I believe my Case was what I find is the Case of most of the wicked Part of the World, *viz*. that to be reduc'd to Necessity is to be wicked; for Necessity is not only the Temptation, but is such a Temptation as human Nature is not empower'd to resist: How good then . . . is that God, which takes from you Sir, the Temptation, by taking away the Necessity?[2]

When Jack asks him whether he would steal again in a similar necessity, the tutor retorts sharply, 'That shews us the Need we have of the Petition of the Lord's-Prayer: *Lead us not into Temptation*; and of *Solomon's*, or *Agar's* Prayer, *Give me not Poverty, least I Steal*. I should ever beg of God not to be left to such Snares as human Nature cannot resist.'[3] He adds

---

[1] *Colonel Jack*, i. 124; i. 188.   [2] Ibid., i. 194.

[3] Ibid., i. 196. It is significant that Defoe put one of the strongest speeches on necessity caused by vice into the mouth of Satan, who urges Sir Richard Steele to attack the government in order to maintain his luxurious way of living: '*And besides*, says the old Prevaricator, *have you not the best Plea in the World for it?* (viz.) *NECESSITY. Prethee*, Dick, says he, *try the other Experiment, can you Starve? You must do one or tother, that you know, there-*

that he hopes he would rather starve than steal, but that since
he is uncertain of his moral 'Strength', he prefers to be removed
from the temptation. His plea is weaker than Jack's, and it is
significant that he neither wins the woman he loves nor gains
as much wealth as the hero.

Jack rewards his tutor, however, and later takes back and
remarries his divorced wife, who, like the tutor, has fallen into
a state of necessity through vice. When the tutor, ignorant of
her former marriage, falls in love with her, they form a triangle
of characters, each embodying some aspect of necessity. This
mingling of love and necessity gives a degree of unity to the
work which is otherwise held together only by Jack's personality
and adventures. Jack remains the main character in the work
long after he has passed the state of danger, but his sympathy
for those who commit crimes because of necessity is a continual
reminder of his early life and problems.

The degree to which this pattern appears in Defoe's other
fiction varies. Captain Singleton experiences a brief period of
necessity as a child, but his later life as a pirate is the result of
squandering his money in luxury. Moll Flanders, on the other
hand, is always searching for some security in marriage from the
poverty which seems to threaten her life. When she is left
destitute at the age of forty-eight, without the charms which
made her a successful wife and mistress, a fear of necessity
and poverty drives her to steal to preserve her life. As her money
diminishes in the three years she lives alone after her husband's
death, Moll sees before her the terrors of starvation. She exclaims:

O let none read this part without seriously reflecting on the Circumstances of a desolate State, and how they would grapple with
want of Friends and want of Bread; it will certainly make them
think not of sparing what they have only, but of looking up to
Heaven for support, and of the wise Man's Prayer, *Give me not
Poverty lest I steal.*[1]

fore Consider of it.' An Essay upon Buying and Selling of Speeches (1716),
p. 22.
    [1] *The Fortunes and Misfortunes of the Famous Moll Flanders*, Shakespeare
Head ed., ii. 3.

Moll appeals to the sympathy of the reader, reminding us that 'a time of Distress, is a time of dreadful Temptation, and all the Strength to resist is taken away'.[1] In this state, which involves a fear of poverty and hunger rather than absolute necessity, Moll is driven to steal.

Looking back on her first theft from her repentant old age, Moll blames the Devil and poverty; but her chief concern at the time is not so much with the morality of the act itself as with the fear that, like Colonel Jack, she might have robbed from a poor widow in the same necessity as herself. Although she finds comfort in the conviction that such a thing would be unlikely, her concern with this particular violation of the law of nature follows a pattern. Eventually, in stealing from a family whose house is on fire, Moll commits this type of crime. Concerning this 'greatest and worst Prize' she remarks, 'I confess the inhumanity of this Action mov'd me very much, and made me relent exceedingly, and Tears stood in my Eyes upon that Subject: But with all my Sense of its being cruel and Inhuman, I cou'd never find in my Heart to make any Restitution'.[2] Moll's guilt is greater than Jack's because although she realizes the extent of her crimes, she refuses either to make restitution or to abandon her way of life. It is suggestive of divine Providence that the next time Moll attempts to steal at a fire, she is struck and almost killed by a mattress which is thrown from a window.

After a few years, Moll becomes a pickpocket and shop-lifter, and she describes herself as 'a compleat Thief, harden'd to a Pitch above all the Reflections of Conscience or Modesty'.[3] This emphasis upon the effect which necessity has upon her is important for a true understanding of her character and the work itself. The men seldom comment upon this hardness because it is more natural to them. But Moll is a woman, and it is only necessity which forces her to assume a role which is basically masculine. Necessity having removed her 'Modesty' she even operates for a while disguised as a man. She upbraids

---

[1] Ibid., ii. 3.   [2] Ibid., ii. 22.   [3] Ibid., ii. 16.

herself for these actions in her narrative, but these moralizings
are the result of her repentance. She tells the reader that when
she first began to steal she feared that she might '... be driven...
to the Gates of Destruction, Soul and Body'.[1] She even suggests
that the Devil prompted her to think of murdering a defenceless
child from whom she steals. But Moll is exaggerating her crimes.
'I had a great many tender Thoughts about me yet', she remarks,
'and did nothing but what, as I may say, meer Necessity drove
me to.'[2] Except for her robbery at the fire, Moll acts with an
impeccable sense of her rights under natural law.

Moll's remorse for her crimes also throws some doubt on her
attempt to plead necessity as an excuse for her actions. At one
point, for instance, she seems to suggest that she might have
abandoned her crimes for a more honest livelihood shortly after
her first few successes:

Thus the Devil who began, by the help of an irresistible Poverty,
to push me into this Wickedness, brought me to a height beyond
the common Rate, even when my Necessities were not so terrifying;
for I had now got into a little Vein of Work, and as I was not at a
loss to handle my Needle, it was very probable I might have got my
Bread honestly enough.[3]

Yet this account does not correspond with an earlier statement
that she 'had little Work, and nothing to live on'.[4] Although this
may be merely carelessness on Defoe's part, it seems to establish a conflict in Moll's mind. As a religious convert she feels
that she ought to condemn her former actions, while her more
genuine and certainly more convincing sentiment seems to be
an attempt to excuse all her actions on the grounds of necessity.

Unlike Jack, however, Moll continues to steal after she is
wealthy enough to retire. Indeed she reminds the reader that
she was 'far from being Poor' and that 'the Temptation of
Necessity, which is the general Introduction of all such Wickedness, was now removed'.[5] Defoe wanted to make this fact very
clear. Not only are we told that Moll is no longer in a state of

[1] *Moll Flanders*, ii. 6.   [2] Ibid., ii. 8.   [3] Ibid., ii. 16.
[4] Ibid., ii. 15.   [5] Ibid., ii. 37.

necessity, but two false speeches on poverty are inserted ironi-cally. 'I assure you', Moll's governess tells the gentleman whom Moll has robbed of both virtue and purse, 'she would never have yielded to you; and as her Poverty first prevail'd with her to let you do as you did, so the same Poverty prevail'd with her to pay her self at last.'[1] Yet the reader knows that Moll is not only wealthy but that she has little virtue to yield. And when she is finally caught, Moll recites a speech on necessity with an ease indicative of frequent rehearsals. 'I gave the Master very good Words', she says, 'told him the Door was open, and things were a Temptation to me, that I was poor, and distress'd, and Poverty was what many cou'd not resist. . . .'[2] The difference between the perfunctory tone of these speeches and the con-viction of Moll's earlier utterances is unmistakable.

Although Defoe's use of necessity as an excuse for theft followed the theories established by the seventeenth-century civilians, his extension of this same doctrine to prostitution seems to have been without precedent. Both Moll Flanders and Roxana become prostitutes, and their excuse is the same as that offered by Defoe as a defence of theft. Moll's career as a pros-titute or mistress begins at Bath, where after returning from America without any money, she becomes the paramour of a gentleman whom she meets there. 'I had the terrible prospect of Poverty and Starving', she tells the reader, 'which lay on me as a frightful Spectre, so that there was no looking behind me: But as Poverty brought me into it, so fear of Poverty kept me in it.'[3] Here, as in her later career as a thief, Moll is motivated more by the 'fear of Poverty' than by the actual experience with extreme necessity.

After being abandoned by her first lover, Moll claims that she would have made an excellent wife for any man, since in her case, 'the Vice came in always at the Door of Necessity, not at the Door of Inclination'.[4] Hence Moll is a complete contrast to the wife of her future husband and business manager whose

[1] Ibid., ii. 52. [2] Ibid., ii. 97. [3] Ibid., i. 125.
[4] Ibid., i. 135.

wife was '. . . a Whore not by Necessity, which is the common
Bait, but by Inclination, and for the sake of the Vice'.[1] Moll does
eventually make a good 'sober' wife to the bank manager and
argues that she would have lived happily and contented for the
rest of her life if he had not died and she had not fallen into
'that Poverty which is the sure Bane of Virtue'.[2] She always
regrets that she did not stop her series of marriages and affairs
after her lover at Bath had shown her the way to repentance.
Not without a certain vanity, she laments the poverty which
forced her to take '. . . Advantage of what they call a handsome
Face' in order to relieve her 'Necessities'.[3] And she adds as a
final moral and excuse for all her actions:

> . . . there are Temptations which it is not in the Power of Human
> Nature to resist, and few know what would be their Case, if driven
> to the same Exigencies: As Covetousness is the Root of all Evil, so
> Poverty is the worst of all Snares.[3]

But while Defoe does allow this plea to excuse prostitution, it
must be concluded once again that her plea is weaker than Jack's.

It is a point in her favour that Moll acts from necessity rather
than lewdness, although her insistence upon her lack of pleasure
seems a strange kind of Puritanism. Over twenty years before,
Defoe wrote in his *True Born Englishman* that prostitution was
almost invariably caused by economic need:

> For where the Vice prevails, the great Temptation
> Is want of Money, more than Inclination.[4]

And in 1726 he attacked Mandeville's theory that prostitution
was rooted in the physical nature of women and therefore inevitable. The real culprit, Defoe believed, was the man, not the
woman. 'Man's Solicitation', he wrote, 'tempts them to Lewdness, Necessity succeeds Sins and Want puts an end to Shame.'[5]
This pattern, however, suggests that Moll's original failure to
resist temptation in her first affair at Colchester was the original

---

[1] *Moll Flanders*, i. 142.   [2] Ibid., i. 202.   [3] Ibid., i. 203.
[4] In *The Shortest Way with the Dissenters*, p. 51.
[5] *Some Considerations upon Street-Walkers*, p. 8.

cause of her downfall. Certainly Defoe placed most of the blame
on her seducer ('if there were no Whore-Masters, there would
be no Whores'), but some of the guilt must reflect on Moll.[1] Her
plea, then, borders on one made for falling into necessity
through vice—a plea which Defoe regarded as untenable.

Both Moll and Roxana are extraordinary women, but whereas
Moll becomes the 'greatest artist' of her time as a thief, she is,
at best, only half-hearted as a prostitute, always seeking a comfortable marriage as the solution to her problems. 'I understood
too well', she remarks, 'by the want of it, what the Value of a
settl'd Life was, to do anything to forfeit the felicity of it.'[2]
Roxana, on the other hand, becomes the 'Queen of Whores'
and after her initial modesty is conquered seems to have been
perfectly satisfied to remain in her profession. The difference
between their attitudes is determined to some extent by their
backgrounds. Whereas Moll was raised in poverty and servitude,
Roxana has been well educated, attended church regularly, and
been accustomed to the comforts of middle-class existence. But
like all of Defoe's heroes and heroines, she is thrown into a state
of necessity through conditions which she cannot control. By
their inclination to crime, Jack, Moll, and Singleton eventually
improve their lot, but for Roxana there seems to be little but
shame in the life she is forced to endure. Yet Defoe refuses to
have his heroine turn her back on life; Defoe rejected suicide
as dying for fear of the 'bitterness of life'.[3] Nor would Defoe
have approved of Roxana's suggestion that she might have been
better off if she had allowed herself to starve to death:

Hitherto I had not only preserv'd the Virtue itself, but the
virtuous inclination and Resolution; and had I kept myself there,
I had been happy, tho' I had perished of meer Hunger; for, without
question, a Woman ought rather to die, than to prostitute her
Virtue and Honour, let the Temptation be what it will.[4]

Writing of the 'fallen tradesman', Defoe remarked that he should
never despair. 'A Man that will lie still, should never hope to

---

[1] *The Anatomy of Exchange-Alley* (1719), p. 26.
[2] *Moll Flanders*, i. 135.   [3] *Family Instructor*, Tegg ed., xv. 381.
[4] *The Fortunate Mistress* (1927), i. 30.

rise'; he warned, 'he that will lie in a Ditch and pray, may
depend upon it he shall lie in the Ditch and die'.[1] And
this speech is an echo of Roxana's comment on her first
husband: 'A Man of Sence falls in the World and gets-up
again, and a Woman has some Chance for herself, but with a
FOOL! once fall and ever undone; once in the Ditch, and die
in the Ditch; once poor, and sure to starve.'[2] Roxana upbraids
herself for prostituting her virtue, but she is no 'FOOL'; and
Defoe would have exonerated her entirely. Her plea of necessity
is actually far stronger than Moll's.

Unlike Moll, who sins at first from the temptations of love
and the desire for wealth, Roxana is entirely guiltless until her
husband's folly, culminating in his desertion of his wife and
children, brings her to a point of extreme necessity. She tells the
reader:

> The House, that was before handsomely furnish'd with Pictures
> and Ornaments, Cabinets, Pier-Glasses, and everything suitable,
> was now . . . seiz'd by the Landlord for Rent or sold to buy Neces-
> saries; in a word, all was Misery and Distress, the Face of Ruin was
> everywhere to be seen; we had eaten up almost everything, and little
> remain'd, unless, like one of the pitiful Women of *Jerusalem*, I
> should eat up my very Children themselves.[3]

In her distress she is forced to send four of her children to
relatives and one to be brought up by the parish in which he was
born. She later upbraids herself for this action, but her argument that 'they must inevitably be Starv'd, and I too, if I
continued to keep them about me' is irrefutable. Roxana
actually shows far greater tenderness for her five offspring than
Moll reveals towards any of her brood but the son born out of
her incestuous marriage. Roxana is comforted by their departure only because she is 'freed from the dreadful Necessity
of seeing them all perish'.[4]

After saving her children as best she can, Roxana is faced

---

[1] *Compleat English Tradesman*, ii. 183.   [2] *Fortunate Mistress*, i. 110.
[3] Ibid., i. 16. For the origins of this scene see *Review*, i. 418a.
[4] Ibid., i. 18.

with the problem of choosing between either death with honour
or a life of disgrace. In a debate between Roxana and her maid,
Amy, Defoe presented the struggle between virtue and necessity
in a manner not very different from the traditional conflict
between the soul and the body. Amy commences by arguing that
the landlord's sudden philanthropy is not entirely without
libidinous motives. Roxana then accuses Amy of cynicism
concerning human benevolence and charity, but Amy's reply
is yet more cynical: 'O, Madam', says Amy, 'there's abundance
of Charity begins in that Vice, and he is not so unacquainted
with things as not to know that Poverty is the strongest incentive; a Temptation against which no Virtue is powerful enough
to stand out.' Apparently surprised by Amy's remarks, Roxana
proclaims that she would rather 'starve' than surrender her
virtue. Amy's retort is stronger: 'I hope not, Madam, I hope
you would be wiser; I'm sure if he will set you up, as he talks
of, you ought to deny him nothing; and you will starve if you
do not consent, that's certain.' Having chosen her first husband
for his excellent dancing ability and handsome appearance,
Roxana, who still holds ideals of romantic love, is shocked by the
thought of prostituting herself for food. Amy, however, insists
that there can be no other justification for yielding. Defoe would
unquestionably have agreed with Amy when she tells Roxana
that prostitution 'would not be Lawful for anything else, but
for Bread'. Amy asserts that wilful starvation is an impossibility;
human nature is frail, and whenever there remains any means
to preserve life, man will grasp at it in spite of virtue and religion.
'As to Honesty', says Amy, 'I think Honesty is out of the
question when Starvation is the Case.'[1]

Of course Roxana gives in at last. In recalling her first transgression, she states that she should have chosen death before
dishonour. She sees Amy as a 'Viper and Engine of the Devil'
and bitterly attacks her own frailty.[2] But she also pleads poverty
as a palliation for her loss of virtue:

. . . my Circumstances were my Temptation; the Terrors behind me

¹ Ibid., i. 27–29.   ² Ibid., i. 40.

look'd blacker than the Terrors before me; and the dreadful Argument of wanting Bread, and being run into the horrible Distresses I was in before, master'd all my Resolution. . . .[1]

Roxana says that she offers this excuse not as a 'Justification' of her sins but to '. . . move the Pity, even of those that abhor the Crime'.[2] She is crueller to herself than Defoe wants his audience to be. When, after she has become mistress of the Prince, Roxana states that she would have sold herself to his footman for 'Bread' just a short time before, the reader knows that this is the exaggeration of a penitent. Amy's doctrine of *'Comply and Live; deny and starve'* has only one logical result—the involuntary drive for survival must conquer.[3]

The Fortunate Mistress is an extraordinarily confusing book because Roxana herself, now a religious convert, refuses to accept Amy's doctrine as a valid excuse. Disturbed by her sinning against her 'Light', by her complete realization of the nature of her crimes, Roxana insists on viewing her past actions in the light of Christian ideals rather than the laws of nature. Although Moll sees the power of the Devil behind many of her sins, she seems satisfied with her plea of necessity. Roxana on the contrary sees the Devil as the cause of her poverty as well as of her temptation and fall:

It occur'd naturally upon this Enquiry, that at first I yielded to the Importunity of my Circumstances, the Misery of which, the Devil dismally aggravated to draw me to comply; for I confess I had strong Natural Aversions to the Crime at first, partly owing to a virtuous Education, and partly to a Sence of Religion; but the Devil, and that greater Devil of Poverty, prevail'd, and the Person who laid Siege to me, did it in such an obliging, and I may almost say irresistible Manner, all still manag'd by the Evil Spirit; for I must be allow'd to believe, that he has a Share in all such things, if not the whole Management of them. . . . These Circumstances, I say, the Devil manag'd, not only to bring me to comply, but he continued them as Arguments to fortify my Mind against all Reflection, and to keep me in that horrid Course, I had engag'd in, as if it were honest and lawful.[4]

---

[1] *Fortunate Mistress*, i. 47.   [2] Ibid., i. 42.   [3] Ibid., i. 197.
[4] **Ibid., ii. 3.**

Roxana realizes that in following what Rousseau called 'the stern law of necessity', she has not been entirely evil, but she also knows that the laws of nature are not always compatible with Christianity.[1] It would be a mistake, however, to confuse Roxana's tortured self-condemnations with a final judgement on her life, since, unlike Jack or Moll, she narrates her story during the anguish and remorse of Christian repentance.

Although almost all of Defoe's characters are Christian penitents they seldom concern themselves with violations of the laws of society. The reason for this is perfectly clear. Natural law was regarded as a divine law of reason, far superior to the unjust and often absurd legal codes of eighteenth-century Europe. But Defoe was a writer of fiction, and the opinions on necessity in his novels are almost always presented by a narrator who was once destitute. Where Defoe depicted respectable members of the middle class or gentry, there is little mention of necessity as a justification for theft. It is not surprising, however, that when the subject is raised among a group of Defoe's middle-class characters, they should condemn necessity as an insufficient reason for allowing a thief to go free; any other opinion would be inconsistent with the social realities of Defoe's era. In his *Religious Courtship*, which may be described as a fictional moral dialogue, an old lady and her two nieces, whose social position and education are approximately the same as Roxana's before her downfall, rehearse the problem of what to do with thieves who, on being caught, plead that 'it was necessity forced them to do what they did'. The nieces concur with their aunt that to let a thief go free would be wrong not only because it was against the law but also because it would make one responsible for any subsequent crime which the thief might commit.[2]

This argument does not indicate a contradiction in Defoe's ideas; it merely suggests that he was not blind to the social implications of his beliefs. Of course Defoe realized that society was obliged to punish malefactors. This, indeed, is one of the lessons of *The Farther Adventures of Robinson Crusoe*. But he

---

[1] *Émile*, p. 47.   [2] Tegg ed., xiv. 322.

also insisted that laws be clear, rational, and just, perceiving the injustice of contemporary English society which failed to provide for the poor, drove them to crime, and then hanged them. No wonder that Defoe's heroes and heroines escape the hangman. None of them fall into necessity through vice; therefore they cannot be charged with guilt for their early crimes. But these acts shade into innumerable social sins. It is usually for these later and more flagrant breaches of morality that Defoe allowed his characters to be punished, not for crimes committed in accordance with the laws of nature.

IV

LOVE, MARRIAGE, AND NATURAL
STANDARDS IN SOCIETY

I

. . . the legislative Authority of our Country never are intended to contradict either the Law of Nature or the Divine Law.

DEFOE, *A Treatise concerning the Use and Abuse of the Marriag Bed*[1]

DEFOE's use of the laws of nature was, as I have shown, not uncommon in his age. But when we turn to the problem of the function of natural law within society, we enter upon a subject which even Grotius and Pufendorf considered ambiguous. Here more than ever the discovery of strange customs in foreign lands clouded the image of man's natural qualities. Although they still regarded their culture as the most advanced, European writers began to wonder if western civilization had not destroyed some of man's natural virtues. Everyone agreed that the 'Divine Law' had improved upon the law of nature; at the same time, there was no longer universal agreement about the lessons which might be drawn from the Bible. If a single, clear standard might be ascertained from natural law, all difficulties would be solved. The problem was that nature seemed so various, and this was especially true in the matters of love and marriage which I intend to discuss in this chapter.

That no single standard might be found is apparent from Pufendorf's discussion of marriage and divorce, which reads like an anthology of opinions. While he may undertake to refute some radical ideas, he refuses to be dogmatic. His conclusion seems to have been that any number of customs might satisfy the bare requirements of natural law. The best policy was for

[1] (1727), p. 125.

every citizen to obey the laws of his society, since it 'would be idle and ridiculous for such Persons, as have not the Power of making or of reversing Civil Laws' to justify disobedience on the law of nature.[1] Like most defenders of monarchy, Pufendorf believed that it was better to endure bad laws than to rebel.

Lacking Pufendorf's dread of rebellion, Defoe created characters who break through the laws of society and religion and ask to be judged at the 'Bar of Nature'. They confess their wickedness, yet they expect to be forgiven for those acts which were committed through human weakness. In examining the rational foundations of these acts and their relation to natural law, we must never forget that Defoe has a vivid sense of evil and that he is always talking of the corrupt law of nature. In much the same manner as Swift in the *Tale of a Tub*, he remarked on the benefits of not being able to see into the human heart:

> How happy . . . is it for the greatest Part of Mankind, that Nature has made no Glass Beehives to the Heart; that it is not in Man to know what is in Man! What a Sink of Wickedness! What a Hell of Treachery and Falshood would be every Day the Subject of our Speculations!
> How many blushing Brides would appear to be rejected—! How many Modest looking Youths would appear distempered, debauched Carcases! How many richly appearing Merchants, to be real Bankrupts! . . . Blessed Fate of Men! How happy are we, that we see no more than the Outsides of one another! And where is the Man who could bear Inspection into the Inside of his Soul?[2]

The problem was to arrive at a standard of justice which would suit man's natural propensity to evil and still be equitable.

Such a standard was obviously difficult to find, especially in matters of love and marriage, where Defoe believed men were ruled less by religion than by uncontrollable passions. 'The Lust of the Flesh', he wrote, 'is so bewitching and natural to the greater part of Mankind, . . . that it hath occasion'd . . . more disorders, and is apter to engage Men over whom it obtains the ascendent in more desperate Undertakings than any other

---

[1] *Law of Nature*, p. 110 (VI. i. 36).   [2] Lee, iii. 179.

passion whatever.'[1] Whereas it was possible to establish a clear contradiction between the law of nature on necessity and the high moral tone of the narrators by referring to both Defoe's didactic writings and the speeches of his fictional characters, no such clarity can be found in his discussion of marriage. He uses natural law as a standard of judgement, but because there is no single rule to follow, it will be necessary to examine each episode and its distinct legal problems if we are to understand it completely.

One thing which we can be certain about is that he avoids any reference to a law of necessity governing sexual problems. In his *Critical Essay concerning Marriage*, Thomas Salmon defended taking a second wife in cases where the first wife had become insane. '*A real Necessity*', he wrote, 'would certainly go a great Way in excusing the Practice; though it be granted, that nothing but an *absolute Necessity* can warrant it.'[2] Defoe, on the contrary, deliberately refused to discuss the question of sexual necessity in his 'Advice from the Scandal Club', and his reply to a bigamist making this plea leaves little doubt about his opinion. No necessity for marriage, he maintained, was uncontrollable. The reason must always be a strict guardian over the 'Preposterous Humour of Love', and where it was not, the emotion was better described as 'Lust'.[3]

Defoe's lengthiest statement concerning the morals of marriage and love is a 'Satyr' on the evils of the age. This means that in the *Treatise concerning the Use and Abuse of the Marriage Bed* he adopts a higher moral tone than he assumed in his novels. Nevertheless it is clear that his normative standard is a 'natural' one, based on the behaviour of animals when he wants to show how the passions should function and on the customs of various savage nations when he wants to illustrate 'natural' reason. The following comparison between mankind and the 'Brutes' is typical:

[1] *Reasons Humbly Offer'd for a Law to Enact the Castration of Popish Ecclesiastics* (1700), p. 20.
[2] (1724), p. 101. See also John Butler, *The True Case of John Butler* (1697), p. 20; and *Concubinage and Polygamy Disprov'd* (1698), p. 19 for a debate on this question.   [3] *Review*, ii. 87*a*; i. 347*a*.

The Brutes obey the Laws of Nature; 'tis not a submission, not a subjection, but a meer Consequence of their Life; and 'tis the manner in which their natural Powers are directed; 'tis the Channel in which they flow; they know their Seasons, and they follow as Nature leads. . . .

But Man! ungoverned Man! neither influenced by the Laws of God, or of Nature, gives himself a loose to his corrupted Desires, and subjects Nature, Reason, and even Religion it self, to his Appetite; in short, to a corrupted and depraved Appetite, a furious outrageous Gust. . . .[1]

Of course Defoe knew that animals did not always follow a law of natural decency. In using animals as a norm to satirize mankind, he was merely doing what Montaigne had already done so well in his 'Apology for Raimond Sebond'.

His use of the savage is also reminiscent of Montaigne. Although Defoe frequently attacked the corruption of primitive nations, in this satire the noble savage is shown obeying a universal law of nature and reason—a law which the evil European has forsaken. For a true image of what marriage should be, western man must observe the American Indian or even the lowly Hottentot. Unlike their prurient, civilized brethren, they regard sex merely as a means of producing children and desist from sexual activity as soon as their wives have conceived.

Let such Men go not to the Forest and the Beasts only, for they act from a much better Motion, but to the more rational, more moderate and better governed Savages of the *Indies*, *East* or *West*, to the Negroes of *Africa*, the Potiguaras's of Brasile, nay to the very Hottentots *Monomotapa*, and the Cape of *Good Hope*; they will find Reason and Nature too prevails among them to act quite otherwise, and while Reason and Nature concur in arming them against it, so they more punctually obey the command of both. . . .[2]

And he added that those who believe there is no rule of modesty to be observed after marriage 'do not rightly consider the Laws of Nature'.[3]

In spite of this appeal to the concept of the noble savage,

---

[1] *Use and Abuse*, p. 294.   [2] Ibid., p. 66.   [3] Ibid., p. 67.

Defoe refused to rely on the consensus of world custom for his standard of natural law, for custom was usually corrupt, whether in Europe or the South Seas. 'Nature we know', he wrote, 'Reason we know, but who are you? You, Custom, you are . . . an Invader of Nature, and an Usurper of the Throne of Reason, that sets up for a Judge of Convenience, and a Judge of Right and Wrong. . . .'[1] Custom, he asserted, is often merely the continuation of crime and gives no justification for a violation of the laws of nature and reason. We may rightly think that Defoe is hedging. How is he to distinguish the laws of nature from custom? Certainly his position is clearer and far less intransigent in his fiction than in his satires.

One concept, however, may be established without reference to his fiction, and this is the idea of true love and the perfect marriage, for on this subject Defoe was surprisingly consistent. Married love ought to be 'founded in Sympathy, nourish'd by Suitability, strengthen'd by Property, and confirm'd by Honesty'.[2] The ideal couple, he maintained, 'are all Love, and because they are all Love, therefore their Behaviour is all Peace; the Calm is in the Soul, and when it is so, there can never be a Storm in the Mind; Love is not in them a Passion but a Quality; 'tis rooted and riveted in their very Beings. . . .'[3] Nor did Defoe always insist on 'Property'. Although prudence is helpful in matters of love, it is not entirely necessary. Such a romantic theory may seem strange indeed for a writer whose fictional characters have so many difficulties with marriage, but, for all his remarks on human corruption, Defoe, like so many satirists, was an idealist at heart. He usually preferred to criticize marriage morality through a device like Colonel Jack's absurd search for a good wife, yet he could not resist one idealization: Robinson Crusoe's wife, as Coleridge remarked, was Defoe's exemplary helpmate.[4]

---

[1] Ibid., p. 300.   [2] *Review*, v. 410b.
[3] *Use and Abuse*, p. 115.
[4] See Samuel Taylor Coleridge, *Miscellaneous Criticism*, ed. Thomas Raysor (1936), p. 298.

II

Chastity is a Virtue much talked of, little practised.
DEFOE, *Treatise concerning the Use and Abuse of the
Marriage Bed*[1]

IN the episode from *Moll Flanders* where Moll meets the gentleman who insists on revealing his self-control by lying naked
beside her, without offering to touch her, Defoe was reflecting
on the impossibility of such a situation continuing long,
especially with Moll's confessing herself to being 'much wickeder
than he'. Moll's reflections on her amazing lover reveal her
bewilderment:

This was a surprising thing to me, and perhaps may be so to
others, who know how the Laws of Nature Work; for he was a
vigorous brisk Person; nor did he act thus on a Principle of Religion
at all, *but of meer Affection*; insisting on it, that tho' I was to him
the most agreeable Woman in the World, yet because he lov'd me
he could not injure me.[2]

Such a noble affection might show love as a 'quality' rather
than a passion, but it was against the laws of nature. 'I own it
was a noble Principle', Moll says doubtfully, but the final moral
which she draws, albeit she is somewhat vague on the fact that
she was the cause of putting an end to this 'perfectly amazing'
virtue, reveals the folly of tempting human nature.[3]

In his *Essay upon Projects*, Defoe proposed an 'academy' for
training women in order to enable them to develop their minds,
which he thought fully equal to those of the men who had
deprived them of all but the simplest education. While he
rejected the rigorously virtuous training which Mary Astell
advocated in her *Serious Proposal to the Ladies* as smacking too
much of a nunnery, he agreed with her that the only means of
preserving the chastity of the students was to exclude men:

. . . for though inclination, which we prettily call love, does sometimes move a little too visibly in the sex, and frailty often follows, yet

[1] *Use and Abuse*, p. 47.   [2] *Moll Flanders*, i. 120.
[3] Ibid., i. 120.

I think, verily, custom, which we miscall modesty, has so far the ascendant over the sex, that solicitation always goes before it.[1]

And he embellished this sentiment with a short poem:

> Custom with women 'stead of virtue rules;
> It leads the wisest and commands the fools;
> For this alone, when inclinations reign,
> Though virtue's fled, will acts of vice restrain.[2]

But without the restraint of a virtuous training, women as well as men are subject to their sexual passions, which have been allowed full freedom by the laws of nature in order to permit mankind to produce offspring. Since 'desires are strong and nature free', virtue in matters of love is not to be expected without the strongest restraints, either the physical restrictions of a cloistered youth or those of 'Custom', by which Defoe meant reputation and all the self-interested ideals of society which masqueraded under the name of modesty.[3]

Pufendorf suggested that men and women also had a natural sense of shame. Yet he admits that this was not a universal quality in regard to nakedness, and his lengthy quotations from a writer named Lambert de Velthuysen demonstrate in ample detail that nudity was not an incentive to lust among the natives of the Indies or of Africa. In spite of this evidence, he persists in the idea that there is a basic sense of shame and modesty which preserves virtue. Bernard Mandeville refined this idea by remarking that while good and evil were imaginary, shame was a very real passion which had been given a particular direction by the customs of European society. 'The Modesty of Women', he wrote, 'is the Result of Custom and Education, . . . the most Virtuous Young Woman alive will often, in spite of her Teeth, have Thoughts and confus'd Ideas of Things arise in her Imagination, which she would not reveal to some People for a Thousand Worlds.'[4] In the same manner, Defoe argued that

---

[1] *Essay upon Projects*, in *The Early Life and Chief Earlier Works*, p. 147.
[2] Ibid., p. 147.
[3] For a similar theory see Pierre Bayle, *Dictionary*, trans. Pierre Desmaizeaux (1734), iii. 814.
[4] *Fable of the Bees*, i. 65.

where nakedness was the social custom, clothing was not necessary to ensure modesty. Friday and his fellow cannibals feel no more shame than Adam before the Fall:

> The same Innocence is the Protection of Virtue to this Day in the untaught Savages in many Parts of the now known World, where Nakedness is no Offence on one side, no Snare, no Incentive on the other; but Custom being the Judge of Decency to them, takes away all Sense of Indecency in going uncovered, whether in whole, or in Part.[1]

But for the European such a return to nudity as a means of regaining the lost innocence of Eden was absurd, 'an Enthusiastick Dream, seldom attempted but by a Sect of Madmen' and leading inevitably to 'all Manner of Lewdness and Debauchery'.[2]

To tempt virtue in this way is to make man into the virtuous being he is not. After the collapse of her virtuous relationship with her Bath gentleman, Moll decides that such experiments with modesty are absurd. 'I have often observ'd since', she warns the reader, '. . . that we ought to be cautious of gratifying our Inclinations in loose and lew'd Freedoms, lest we find our Resolutions of Virtue fail us in the Juncture when their Assistance should be most necessary.'[3] For all his claims, the virtue of Moll's gentleman is a contradiction of human corruption and cannot be sustained for long.

III

O Eve! black was the Guilt that thou wast in!
Or else the Curse is greater than the Sin.
DEFOE, *Good Advice to the Ladies*[4]

THE curse to which Defoe was referring was that of matrimony and the fate of women with bad husbands. Although he knew that marriage was the only lawful way to satisfy natural desires, Defoe could not but lament the existence of a passion which

---

[1] *Use and Abuse*, p. 2.   [2] Ibid., p. 3.
[3] *Moll Flanders*, i. 124.   [4] (1702), p. 7.

usurped the place of reason and so often brought men and women into misery. The only explanation for this condition was original sin:

> It is true, that there is a corrupt Principle inbred and indwelling, taking a kind of Possession, too much in Man's Nature, degenerated as it is by the Fall; this corrupt Principle dictates the Propagation of the Kind, that is, as a Law of Nature, but does it without regard to the limitations imposed by Heaven upon the Branches; that is to say, without entering into the Engagements of Matrimony, and thus makes those Actions criminal, which otherwise would have been lawful. . . .[1]

But though the act of marriage satisfied the positive laws, it did not necessarily satisfy either natural or divine law, for the vices of men and women were not to be controlled by the mere existence of a legal marriage. As one critic has already shown, Defoe's fictional treatment of his characters' marriage problems was intricately involved with questions of contemporary reform of the common law.[2] What I am concerned with, however, is his use of the laws of nature as a corrective for the common law in matters of marriage and divorce.

Perhaps Defoe defined marriage most clearly in the *Farther Adventures*, where Crusoe and the priest discuss the condition of the five Englishmen who have taken native wives. These women were originally brought over to the island as slaves, and when the Spanish governor asks the men whether they will take them as wives or servants, '. . . One of the *Englishmen* answer'd very boldly and readily, That they would use them as both'.[3] The governor sees the difficulties in this, but he merely suggests a contract by which each man will have only one woman while he is on the island. Such an agreement is not a marriage, because it is not made between equals and because there is no provision concerning mutual duties. Grotius treated this relationship as 'concubinage', and although he agreed that

---

[1] *Use and Abuse*, p. 60.
[2] See Spiro Peterson, 'The Matrimonial Theme of Defoe's "Roxana" ', *PMLA*, lxx (1955), 166–91.
[3] *Robinson Crusoe*, ii. 188.

H

such a union was acceptable in the state of nature, he questioned whether a true marriage could be contracted where both parties were not free.[1]

The priest insists that these are not marriages, since the contract involved 'no Agreement with the Women, as Wives, but only an Agreement among themselves, to keep them from quarrelling'.[2] He then advances his own definition of matrimony:

> But, Sir, the Essence of the Sacrament of Matrimony (so he call'd it, being a *Roman*) consists not only in the mutual Consent of the Parties to take one another, as *Man and Wife*, but in the formal and legal Obligation, that there is in the Contract, to compel the Man and Woman at all Times, to own and acknowledge each other, obliging the Men to abstain from all other Women, to engage in no other Contract while these subsist; and on all Occasions, as Ability allows, to provide honestly for them and their Children, and to oblige the Women to the same, or like Conditions, *mutatis mutandis*, on their Side.[3]

According to the priest's exposition of the divine law, the five Englishmen are living in adultery. Crusoe is not in entire agreement, but he does admit

> . . . it was certainly true, that tho' they had no Clergyman upon the Spot, yet a formal Contract on both Sides, made before Witnesses, and confirm'd by any Token, which they had all agreed to be bound by, tho' it had been but breaking a Stick between them, engaging the Men to own these Women for their Wives, upon all Occasions, and never to abandon them or their Children, and the Women to the same with their Husbands, had been an effectual lawful Marriage in the Sight of God; and it was a great Neglect that it was not done.[3]

On this matter both the law of nature and the divine law were in agreement. Very much in accord with Crusoe's concern for written contracts, however, the priest insists on an official document '. . . sign'd by both Man and Woman, and by all the Witnesses present, which all the Laws of *Europe* would decree to be valid'.[4]

---

[1] *De Jure Belli ac Pacis*, ii. 247 (II. v. 15).
[2] *Robinson Crusoe*, iii. 19.
[3] Ibid., iii. 20.   [4] Ibid., iii. 21.

Locke's definition of marriage as 'a voluntary compact between man and woman' explains precisely why the Englishmen are not married.[1] Since they have taken women who have had no opportunity to resist, only the men have acted voluntarily. That Defoe should have introduced such technical legal material into his fiction may seem strange, but he appears to have been fascinated by this subject. He was especially interested in the contrast between marriage under the law of nature where any number of contracts might be valid and marriage under the positive laws where only certain contracts were 'authentick'.

Unfortunately it is frequently impossible to tell if he is appealing to natural law, positive law, or divine law. For example, he argued that a promise, whether made before witnesses or in private, was equivalent to marriage since it had the power of an oath before God. Such an attitude towards conscience may appear to be strictly religious, but we must remember that Defoe would have regarded fidelity to an oath as part of the law of nature as well. Speaking for the Scandal Club in reply to a correspondent who had complained that he only promised to marry a woman to prevent her from committing suicide, he defined marriage as

. . . nothing but a Promise, the Ceremony is no Addition to the Contract, only a Thing expected by the Law, to prevent Knaves doing what seems here to be attempted, and therefore the Society insist upon it, when the Promise was made, the Man and Woman were actually Marryed; and he can never go off from it, nor Marry any other Woman; but he must break all the Constitutions of the Marriage Contract, the Sanction of the Law excepted.[2]

And he added the ironic postscript that since the promise was made to save the life of the woman, '. . . she ought to be a very Obliging, Tender, Dutiful, and loving Wife'.[2] By the laws of God and nature, even the rashest oath is sacred, and a promise carries as much obligation as a written contract.

This does not mean that Defoe ignored the importance of

[1] *Two Treatises*, p. 155.　　　[2] *Review*, I, supplement iii. 196.

the written document, but he regarded it as a necessary evil in a corrupt world. One of his favourite paradoxes concerns the dilemma of the woman who allows herself to be seduced before marriage. If the man refuses to marry her, she has a '*Knave for a spark*', but if he consents, then she gains '*a Fool for a Husband*'.[1] This theme appears several times in the *Review* and a variation of it may be found in *Moll Flanders*. Moll's first lover, for example, makes a verbal promise of marriage, which she later tries to convince him is a binding contract. She is fully aware, however, that she had made a mistake in not asking for a legal marriage and that her lover never repeated his proposal after she became his mistress. In a sense, no promise has been broken, for his proposal entailed an important condition: he tells Moll that he would marry her 'as soon as he came to his Estate'. When he argues later that he has 'not broken one Promise' and that he might not fall heir to the estate for another thirty years, his arguments seem to have some weight.[2] But as Thomas Salmon pointed out, such a conditional marriage becomes a real marriage when the couple have lived together as man and wife.[3] Thus Moll is entirely correct when she tells him that she was as much his wife 'as if we had been publickly Wedded by the Parson of the Parish' and upbraids him for contradicting himself:

I told him, he knew very well, I had no Consent to give; and that he had ingag'd himself to marry me, and that I was therby ingag'd to him; that he had all along told me, I was his Wife, and I look'd upon my self as effectually so, as if the Ceremony had pass'd; and that it was from his own Mouth that I did so, he having all along persuaded me to call my self his Wife.[4]

Her arguments are impeccable by the standard of divine and natural law, but they have no effect on her lover, who may be a knave but is certainly no fool. When he threatens to expose their relationship and cast her out of the house, Moll has no choice but to accept the inevitable. Her lover slips out of the

[1] *Review*, i. 243*a*.   [2] *Moll Flanders*, i. 24, 35.
[3] *Critical Essay concerning Marriage*, p. 188.
[4] *Moll Flanders*, i. 32, 36.

contract with Moll's reluctant consent, and thus her first 'natural' marriage ends.

Moll learns something very definite about life in society from this affair—that whereas a contract of marriage in a state of nature may be dissolved by the consent of the two parties, if there are no children to worry about, in society a man might be forced to abide by a written contract. Having learned this lesson, she tricks two men into formal marriages with her by pretending to have more money than she actually has. It is true that both of these turn out badly, but not for any lack of prudence on Moll's part.

These marriages reveal Moll's increased knowledge of the world, but they were illegal, since she was still married to her second husband, the '*Land-water-thing*, call'd, a *Gentleman Tradesman*', who had deserted her after spending most of her money.[1] Her empirical assumption that desertion constitutes divorce, however, had strong support from writers on natural law. Pufendorf contended that since the end of marriage was 'the procuring of Children . . ., if we regard barely the Law of Nature, either Person may quit and renounce the Relation, in case the other prove guilty of base Desertion. . . .'[2] This is essentially the same argument which Amy, who, as we have seen, is well versed in all aspects of natural law, presents to Roxana in urging her to 'marry' the landlord after her husband has deserted her:

. . . he calls you Widow, and such indeed you are; for as my Master has left you so many Years, he is dead to be sure; at least he is dead to you; he is no Husband, you are, and ought to be free to marry who you will; and his [the landlord's] Wife being gone from him, and refuses to lye with him, then he is a single Man again, as much as ever; and though you cannot bring the Laws of the Land to join you together, yet one refusing to do the Office of a Wife, and the other of a Husband, you may certainly take one another fairly.[3]

Refusing to be convinced by this point of natural law, Roxana

[1] Ibid., i. 59. [2] *Law of Nature*, p. 90 (VI. i. 21).
[3] *Fortunate Mistress*, i. 39.

tells Amy that her arguments are 'all Nonsense' and insists on calling herself a 'Whore'.

In spite of Roxana's scepticism, the Landlord persists in giving her a written contract, which treats her not as a mistress but as a wife:

... he showed me a Contract in Writing, wherein he engag'd himself to me; to cohabit constantly with me; to provide for me in all Respects as a Wife; and repeating in the Preamble a long account of the Nature and Reason of our living together, and an Obligation in the Penalty of 7000. l. never to abandon me; and at last showed me a Bond for 500. l. to be paid to me, or to my Assigns within three Months after his Death.[1]

Defoe's lists and contracts have too often been assigned to the limbo of middle-class book-keeping. There can be no question that Roxana was entitled to marry her landlord according to the laws of nature, and she confesses her love for this generous man who rescues her from starvation and offers her his protection. She may have little faith in the legality of this marriage, but it cannot be said that the landlord has not tried his best in the face of an inhumane system of law.

Once she has conquered her doubts about the moral propriety of her liaison, Roxana becomes an ardent advocate of complete equality of the sexes in marriage. At times she seems to be a defender of what was known as an 'Amazonian' marriage, in which the woman assumed control of the children.[2] Although Pufendorf had argued that the sexes were 'naturally equal in Right' and that any surrender of rights had to be a 'free Act', Roxana's attitude shocks the conventional Dutch merchant who has just confidently proposed to her:

I told him, I had, perhaps differing Notions of Matrimony, from what the receiv'd Custom had given us of it; that I thought a Woman was a free Agent, as well as a Man, and was born free, and, cou'd she manage her self suitably, might enjoy that Liberty to as much Purpose as the Men do; that the Laws of Matrimony were indeed, otherwise, and Mankind at this time, acted quite upon other Prin-

---

[1] *Fortunate Mistress*, i. 45.   [2] See Salmon, p. 79.

ciples; and those such, that a Woman gave herself entirely away from herself, in Marriage, and capitulated only to be, at best, but *an Upper-Servant*. . . .[1]

And she shows her true Amazonian colours when she asserts that this freedom applies to sex as well as economics. Roxana later admits that her extreme attitude on this subject was a pretence and that, in her desire to retain control of her wealth, she decided to support her position with some of the most extreme arguments of the natural law philosophers. For the Amazonian marriage, though 'natural' in so far as it seemed to operate without inconvenience in certain areas of the world, was entirely unacceptable to western thought. Pufendorf called it 'Barbarous at least, if not Beastly', and Pierre Bayle, conceding that such marriages were common throughout the world, suggested that, as far as Europe was concerned, 'Things are very well as they are.'[2]

There is no question about Defoe's opinion on this matter. Although he thought that women were worse off in marriage than men, he regarded marriage as a question of sovereignty, with the woman ruling during the engagement and the man after the wedding. He was probably sympathetic to Roxana's unwillingness to surrender her sovereignty in a cruel world, but would have accused her of 'Inverting the Order of her Sex'.[3] The merchant's reply to Roxana, that 'Marriage was decreed by Heaven; that it was the fix'd State of Life which God had appointed for Man's Felicity, and for establishing a Legal Posterity; . . . that all the rest was sunk under Scandal and Illegitimacy . . .', was also Defoe's reply. 'Very well he talk'd upon the Subject, indeed', she admits, even though she refuses to surrender her freedom and wealth for the uncertainties of wedlock.[4]

---

[1] *Fortunate Mistress*, i. 171. Cf. Pufendorf, *Law of Nature*, p. 78 (VI. i. 9).
[2] See Pufendorf, *Law of Nature*, p. 78 (VI. i. 9); and Bayle' *Dictionary*, v. 31.
[3] *Review*, i. 392a. See also *A Collection of Miscellany Letters*, iv. 1–6.
[4] *Fortunate Mistress*, i. 176.

IV

... Mr. *Milton's* Arguements go a great way with me; for, in short, if my wife and I,—by mere agreeing upon Terms,—came together and married,—why may not my wife and I,—by the like mere agreeing upon Terms,— separate again? For if mutual Consent be the Essence of the Contract of Matrimony, why should not the dissolving that mutual Consent dissolve likewise the Marriage and disengage the Parties from one another again?

DEFOE, *Applebee's Journal* (24 April 1725)[1]

SINCE Defoe frequently rejected Milton's ideas on divorce as having too little of 'Scripture Arguements', it would be rash to identify his views too closely with the correspondent to *Applebee's Journal*, but he probably would have agreed that Milton's thesis was perfectly rational when considered from the standpoint of natural law. Even more extreme in its implications than Milton's theories was Locke's suggestion that in the state of nature, marriage ties were binding only so long as the children needed care, and, as we have seen, Pufendorf contended that either party might renounce the marriage in case of 'base Desertion' or of 'Voluntary and Obstinate Unkindness, as to the affair of the Bed'. The reason for this, he explained, arises not from any divine law but from the 'Nature of Covenants'. In the marriage contract, as in all other contracts, when one party breaks the agreement, the other is no longer obliged to keep it, and Pufendorf maintained that 'whatever the *Cannonists* urge to the contrary' the injured person might remarry. He admitted that in a commonwealth the laws of marriage might contradict natural law, but it was unreasonable to expect such laws to be obeyed. These positive laws are unjust because they punish the innocent and the guilty alike and force the deserted spouse to remain in a 'probably inconvenient, perhaps intolerable' state of celibacy.[2]

A reform in the laws on divorce was especially important for women. Thomas Salmon, for instance, wanted such legislation

[1] Lee, iii. 379.   [2] Pufendorf, *Law of Nature*, pp. 91–92 (VI. i. 22).

'not for Men, but to release afflicted Wives', and he attacked the 'senseless Cruelty' which drove women like Moll and Roxana to sin and crime.[1] After Moll's gentleman-tradesman deserts her, she hardly knows what to do. 'I was limited from Marriage', she remarks, 'what Offer soever might be made me.'[2] Eventually, however, she discards this unreasonable scruple and sets out to find another husband, and when her Lancashire husband leaves her, he releases her unconditionally from the contract. *'Our Marriage is nothing'*, he writes, *'I shall never be able to see you again; I here discharge you from it; if you can marry to your Advantage do not decline it on my Account; I here swear to you on my Faith, . . . I will never disturb your Repose if I should know of it. . . .'*[3] Moll takes his advice and marries as soon as she can. Amy offers similar advice concerning desertion and divorce to Roxana, supporting her arguments with references to the customs of other nations which follow the laws of nature more strictly than England. Although Roxana says that the advice came from 'a Viper and Engine of the Devil', even her errant husband maintains that a woman should be permitted to re-marry after four years if her husband has not been heard from.[4]

If deserted wives suffer most of all from unjust divorce laws, the men are not without problems either. Colonel Jack's quest for an honest wife may be absurd, but his difficulties in obtaining divorces are not. Scrupulous enough about his first unfaithful wife to obtain a legal divorce, Jack does not even bother about a legal separation when his second wife proves false. He considers the moral impropriety of this before he is about to marry for a third time. Since his wife has been unfaithful, he knows that a divorce is possible, yet he cannot return to France, where he has violated the law against duelling. Faced with such theoretical difficulties, Defoe's narrators seldom hesitate. Jack merely decides that he might consider himself 'as much divorc'd as if it had been actually done', and by relying on the

---

[1] *Critical Essay concerning Marriage*, p. 139.
[2] *Moll Flanders*, i. 63.   [3] Ibid., i. 162.
[4] *Fortunate Mistress*, i. 103.

efficacy of the laws of nature, he puts aside whatever doubts he may have had.[1]

Defoe evidently decided to adjust his story to some of the laws of probability required by realistic fiction, but the title page promises something closer to the story of a correspondent to *Applebee's*. Tom Manywife has married ten times, never been divorced, never found an honest woman, but is searching for an eleventh wife, although all his former wives are still alive. This man may be said to have solved his problems by ignoring the law entirely. Those who cannot arrive at such a simple solution must try to adjust their lives as well as they can. Like Jane Eyre's suitor, Rochester, Moll's Bath gentleman is saddled with an insane wife from whom he cannot obtain a divorce. And Moll's honest bank manager is married to an adulteress. Here, as in the problem of necessity, Defoe was treating a situation in which the positive laws failed to satisfy the demands of nature and reason. For all their hesitation, Jack, Moll, and Roxana eventually decide to obey the injunction of the Age of Reason: they follow nature.

IV

And presently, as if she had taken me for a Member of Parliament, she explained herself, and told me, if the Parliament would but make a Law by which all the Men should be obliged to marry two Wives, that would effectually cure it.

DEFOE, *Applebee's Journal* (10 April 1725)[2]

SINCE he is a practising polygamist himself, it is not surprising that Tom Manywife should be persuaded that there was some worth in an argument proposing a more rational distribution of wives:

I laugh'd at the Proposal you may suppose, but she went on with her Explanation for all that, and held me in a long Discourse about it, proving the Lawfulness of it,—but especially the Convenience of

---

[1] *Colonel Jack*, ii. 67.   [2] Lee, iii. 375.

it; and in short, that there was no other Way to put a stop to the Wickedness of the Age, and to prevent Lewdness, which was grown up to such an extravagant Height, as that there were few Honest Women, she said, to be found.[1]

Strangely enough, Manywife tells her that 'it was against the Protestant Principles, nay against the Christian Religion' and that they lived in a nation where all the laws were 'squar'd by the great Rules of Religion'. But these high principles are no solution to the woman's lament that only half the ladies in England would ever be married.[1]

Like Tom Manywife's friend, Defoe often complained that a law should be passed to force men to marry, and he ascribed the increase in prostitution to '. . . that Neglect of Matrimony which the Morals of the present Age inspire Men with. . . '.[2] Polygamy, however, was not one of the many panaceas which he suggested as a cure for this problem. His attitude is reflected in the hesitant recognition which the civilians granted to the 'naturalness' of polygamy. Pufendorf, for example, while rejecting polyandry as a perversion of marriage, went so far as to admit that polygamy was practised by many nations of the world including the ancient Jews, but, like Montesquieu in the *Persian Letters*, he objected that no woman would surrender her freedom voluntarily in order to be subjected to the slavery of a harem. He also agreed with Grotius that polygamy probably did not work well and that those nations which, following divine or positive laws, had declared it a form of adultery were better off. Nevertheless, almost everyone admitted that polygamy could hardly be called adultery except in a very broad sense.

In his *Review*, Defoe took a high tone with both adulterers and polygamists, always referring to the divine and common law, almost never to the law of nature. And when he does refer to natural law when discussing polygamy and adultery in his *Use and Abuse of the Marriage Bed*, it is to argue that they were

[1] Ibid., iii. 375.
[2] *Some Considerations upon Street-Walkers*, p. 6. For a survey of opinions on polygamy during the eighteenth century see A. Owen Aldridge, 'Polygamy and Deism', *JEGP*, xlviii (July 1949), 343–60.

the product of corrupt and unnatural customs. Yet there is a certain sympathy in his account of a young man who, being forced by his avaricious father to marry for money, first married his true love and finally decided to live with both wives.[1] Again, in the *General History of the Pyrates*, he remarks that the practice of polygamy among the pirates on Madagascar was not half so bad as some marriage customs among people who pretended to be more civilized.[2] We may conclude from this that although Defoe did not approve of polygamy, he did not regard it as the worst of sins.

Although both Colonel Jack and Moll Flanders are bigamists, only Roxana, whose very name is suggestive of harems, indulges in polygamy. In a strangely perverse mood, she forces her maid, Amy, to go to bed with the landlord and thereby take upon herself some of her mistress's shame. Indeed Roxana seems determined to convince Amy and her lover that the contract which she has signed is anything but a real marriage. As a result of this act, the landlord takes an immediate aversion to Amy and cannot endure her presence. Roxana comes to regard this as her greatest crime, and Defoe seems to be telling his readers that polygamy was unnatural in spite of Roxana's attempt to convince her lover that it was sanctioned by the Bible. 'Come, my dear', she tells him, '. . . when *Rachel* put her Handmaid to Bed to *Jacob* she took the Children as her own; don't be uneasie. . . .' But the landlord is 'uneasie', and Roxana shamefully admits that she was '. . . the Cause of all the Wickedness between them, encourag'd them both when they had any Remorse about it, and rather prompted them to go on with it than to repent of it'.[3]

Roxana forces the landlord to conquer an aversion to Amy which is as natural as Moll's aversion to an incestuous relationship. Here again Defoe was taking a more definite stand than most of the writers on natural law. In the *Review* he had advised a man engaged in an incestuous affair that he was on the sure road to 'Hell'. Such affairs last only

---

[1] *Use and Abuse of the Marriage Bed*, p. 196.   [2] ii. 395.
[3] *Fortunate Mistress*, i. 52.

... while the Causes of them last; and when either the Lust, or the Self-Interest, or the rash Passion ceases, the Affection must wear off, and be cloy'd of Course; for no Love can continue constant, but that which being founded upon Merit in the Person Loved, and Vertue in the Person Loving, has both a Right Beginning and a proper Object, both perhaps are suggested at first, but as the Delusion wears off, the Affection dwindles into Aversion.[1]

On this question, Pufendorf quoted the opinion of Velthuysen, who had contended in his *Epistolica Dissertatio de Principiis Justi et Decori* that 'no *Degrees* of Marriage are forbidden by the Law of Nature; tho' to abstain from some is most agreeable to Natural Honesty'.[2] Pufendorf admitted that he could not help but agree, confessing that many countries which made some pretence to civilization practised incest and that the repugnance which the European felt might arise 'not so much from any in-bred Principle, as from long Use and Custom, which often counterfeit Nature'. In such cases, he argued, it is necessary to put aside our immediate prejudices and 'Affections' in order to judge according to 'Reason and Nature'.[3] Although Pufendorf's final judgement is that men *do* have an inner sense of delicacy and shame, he asserts this as a personal faith and makes no effort to refute the evidence for incestuous societies in Greece and Ceylon.[4]

Like Pufendorf, Defoe shows little respect for the customs of other nations where they seem to contradict his preconception of the law of nature. Thus he fell back on the traditional division between natural law and the 'Law of Nations', which he defined as the individual customs of each society. The laws of nature, he argued, are clear in spite of the corruptions which inevitably invade every society. Custom may usurp the throne of reason temporarily, but it can never entirely extinguish the light of reason inherent in every man.

---

[1] *Review*, v. 27a.   [2] *Law of Nature*, p. 100 (VI. i. 30).
[3] Ibid., p. 98 (VI. i. 28).
[4] Ibid., p. 98 (VI. i. 29). Grotius also admitted that by the 'pure law of nature', incest could not be considered wrong, although the divine law overruled the law of nature on this question. See *De Jure Belli ac Pacis*, ii. 242–3 (II. v. 13).

This same light of reason and nature may be seen operating in the soul of Moll Flanders. She tells the reader that she had not 'the least Affection' for Robin, her first legal husband, and after his death, she confesses, 'I was not suitably affected with the loss of my Husband; nor can I say, that I ever lov'd him as I ought to have done, or was suitable to the good Usage I had from him. . . .'[1] Judged by the rules of her society, there was nothing wrong with this marriage, but Moll retains her affection for Robin's brother and regards her marriage as both incestuous and adulterous. She has a similar aversion to her third legal husband, whom she discovers to be her half brother. '. . . I liv'd therefore in open and avowed Incest and Whoredom', says Moll, 'and all under the appearance of an honest Wife; and tho' I was not much touched with the Crime of it, yet the Action had something in it shocking to Nature, and made my Husband even nauseous to me.'[2] At first she conceals her knowledge from her husband, but, unable to endure this 'unnatural' relationship, she finally reveals her secret.

Moll decides that the only thing she can do is to return to England, but her husband, after recovering from an unsuccessful attempt at suicide and a subsequent illness, urges her to stay. Since no one knows of their secret, he reasons with her, there can be little harm in it. He even accuses Moll of being an 'unnatural Mother' for wanting to leave her children.[3] But these accusations can be dismissed. Moll is probably the best barometer we have for judging the natural climate of Defoe's novels. For Defoe, incest was a violation of the laws of God and nature. Moll may follow her self-interest in most aspects of life, but, incapable of enduring an incestuous marriage, she prefers poverty in England to a life of physical comfort and moral horror in Virginia.

Compared with these sins, prostitution and concubinage seem relatively mild. Because of the difficulties involved in obtaining a divorce, concubines or '*Inferior Wives*' were becoming an established institution and their legal status some-

---

[1] *Moll Flanders*, i. 57.   [2] Ibid., i. 91.   [3] Ibid., i. 93.

thing of a problem. Both Moll and Roxana become concubines, even though Roxana's landlord tries his best to convince her that she is really his wife. In discussing this subject, Thomas Salmon argued that those who lived in pagan nations might still practise concubinage without any violation of the law of nature. 'Where a Positive Law is not sufficiently promulg'd', he wrote, 'it would be hard to punish the Transgression of it, when it is acknowledged not to be contrary to the Law of Nature.'[1] Although Defoe was careful not to confuse concubinage with a legal marriage, like Salmon, he seemed to have regarded it as perfectly natural. Moll's Bath gentleman is unable to marry her, but his affection meets all the qualifications which Defoe insisted upon as the test of true love; and only the irrational positive laws prevent him from marrying her. Yet these laws cannot be dismissed entirely, and in spite of Moll's attempt to make a case for her virtue, she is not very convincing. As Pufendorf argued, even the most faithful concubines 'differ only in Degree from common Strumpets'.[2] Moll is always trying to extract money from her lover in preparation for the inevitable day when her gentleman's love will turn to hatred.

A somewhat similar situation may be found in the *Fortunate Mistress*, where the Prince, in addition to Roxana, has several mistresses and a long-suffering, patient wife. Roxana justifies her life of sin on the basis of love, arguing that 'Heaven would not suffer us to be punish'd for that which it was not possible for us to avoid'.[3] It is doubtful that Defoe would have agreed with this uncharacteristically romantic speech, but he probably felt that she was less guilty than her lover. The sermons which Moll and Roxana preach concerning the evils of concubinage may appear hypocritical, but if we examine them closely, we shall see that they are directed mainly at the folly of men rather than at any self-justification. Roxana tells the reader:

. . . I am a standing Mark of the Weakness of Great Men, in their

[1] *Critical Essay concerning Marriage*, p. 109 [342].
[2] *Law of Nature*, p. 109 (VI. i. 26).
[3] *Fortunate Mistress*, i. 78. She immediately refers to these sentiments as 'Absurdities'.

Vice; that value not squandering away immense Wealth, upon the most worthless Creatures; or, to sum it up in a Word, they raise the Value of the Object which they pretend to pitch upon by their Fancy . . ., give vast Presents for a ruinous Favour, which is so far from being equal to the Price, that nothing will, at last, prove more absurd, than the Cost Men are at to purchase their own Destruction.[1]

And she insists that the entire reason for telling her story is to show how love 'dethrones' the reason in man, '. . . exalts Sence into the vacant Throne; how he deposes the Man, and exalts the Brute'.[2]

Although we must not confuse Roxana's intentions with Defoe's, he probably regarded much of his fiction as a form of 'Satyr' or criticism of the vice and immorality of his time. At the end of his long treatise on marriage, he defended his work on these grounds:

Satyr can scourge where the Lash of the Law cannot; the Teeth and Talons of the Pen will bite and tear; and the Satyr has a Sting which is made for the Correction of such Offences and such Offenders as bully Justice, and think themselves out of the reach of Prisons and Punishments.[3]

An admirer of Juvenal rather than Horace, Defoe wrote a form of satire which was more often lashing than amusing. But unlike most eighteenth-century satirists who appealed to a general and vague concept of nature for their norm, Defoe relied on the more specific ideals of natural law.

---

[1] *Fortunate Mistress*, i. 83.
[2] Ibid., i. 85.   [3] *Use and Abuse of the Marriage Bed*, p. 382 [362].

V

THE WORST OF CRIMES AND THE
MEANING OF GRATITUDE

Ingratitude, a Devil of *Black Renown*,
Possess'd her very early for his own,
An Ugly, Surly, Sullen, Selfish Spirit,
Who Satan's *worst Perfections does Inherit*:
Second to him in Malice and in Force,
All *Devil without*, and all *within* him *Worse*.

DEFOE, *The True Born Englishman*[1]

A LARGE part of the *True Born Englishman* was devoted to
the familiar contemporary literary pastime of sketching the
ruling passions of every nation. In selecting ingratitude as the
special vice of England, Defoe was accusing his country of a far
worse crime than the lust of Italy or the drunkenness of Ger-
many. In his influential work, *The Passions of the Soul*, Descartes
refused to recognize ingratitude as a passion, concluding that
it was merely a 'vice directly opposed to gratitude',[2] and in
Lilliput, as Gulliver informs us, ingratitude was a capital
offence, 'For they reason thus; that whoever makes ill Returns
to his Benefactor, must needs be a common Enemy to the rest
of Mankind, from whom he hath received no Obligation; and
therefore such a Man is not fit to live'.[3] We may safely dismiss
Defoe's surprise at the attacks made against him for abusing the
national character as a mask of innocence which satirists
frequently assume when answering their enemies. But if

---

[1] In *The Shortest Way with the Dissenters*, p. 36.

[2] *The Philosophical Works*, trans. Elizabeth Haldane and G. R. T. Ross
(1955), i. 418. Pierre Charron described it as '. . . an Offence against
Nature, and a certain indication of an Ill Temper; a scandalous and re-
proachful Vice; such as is not to be endured, because it breaks all Society
and good Correspondence'. See *Of Wisdom*, trans. George Stanhope (1707),
ii. 216 (III. xi. 19).

[3] Jonathan Swift, *Gulliver's Travels, Prose Works*, ed. Herbert Davis
(1959), xi. 60.

ingratitude was the most unnatural of sins, gratitude could be a dangerous virtue, for it was so natural and so strong an emotion that it might lead to the destruction of other moral principles. For the characters in Defoe's fiction, who function in a world of natural values, gratitude is a central virtue, and Defoe sometimes tested his protagonists by placing them in paradoxical situations involving the obligation between women and their lovers, citizens and their country, and parents and their children.

Gratitude was not only one of Defoe's literary themes but also involved a personal creed. When he was in prison, Harley wrote to Godolphin that Defoe was so 'much oppress'd in his mind' that an act of kindness might '. . . engage him better than any after rewards, and keep him more under the power of an obligation'.[1] Harley made a shrewd guess. Apparently Defoe felt this obligation deeply, and years later he was still reminding his patron of his gratitude. '. . . My Services (However Small) are founded Rather *and indeed Entirely* on a Deep Sence of Duty and Gratitude for that Early goodness, Than on any View that I can Merit what may be to Come', he wrote to Harley in 1712.[2] And in his *Appeal to Honour and Justice* he chose to rest almost his entire 'appeal' to his audience on this single virtue:

Gratitude and Fidelity are inseparable from an honest Man. But to be thus oblig'd by a Stranger, by a Man of Quality and Honour, and after that by the Sovereign, under whose Administration I was suffering, let any one put himself in my stead, and examine upon what Principles I could ever act against either such a Queen, or such a Benefactor; and what must my own Heart reproach me with, what blushes must have cover'd my Face when I had look'd in, and call'd myself ungrateful to him that sav'd me thus from distress? or Her that fetch'd me out of the Dungeon, and gave my Family Relief? Let any Man, who knows what Principles are, what Engagements of Honour and Gratitude are, make this Case his own, and say what I could have done less or more than I have done.[3]

[1] *Historical Manuscripts Commission*, 8th report (1907), i. 43b.
[2] *Letters of Daniel Defoe*, ed. George Healey (1955), p. 379.
[3] In *The Shortest Way with the Dissenters*, p. 201.

I am not suggesting that this is a valid excuse for the erratic course of Defoe's changing allegiances, although he probably felt more loyalty to Harley than to any abstract principle. What is interesting for our purposes is that he would lean so heavily on gratitude (he dismisses necessity in this work as a dangerous plea in politics) as an excuse for committing whatever wrongs his enemies might charge him with.

'GRATITUDE', he once wrote, 'never dyes, and Obligation never ceases; nothing can wear it out of the Mind, where the Mind is once possess'd with Principles of Honour, of Religion, and of Justice: A Man of Honour can no more be Ingrate, than a Man of Honesty can Steal.'[1] But while a sense of gratitude may be heightened by these civilized values, it is basically a natural virtue, and probably the dominant virtue of Defoe's noble savage. In *A New Voyage round the World*, the narrator is delighted by a display of gratitude on the part of one of the savages, and when Crusoe saves the life of Friday's father, he describes how the cannibal looked at him '. . . with all the Tokens of Gratitude and Thankfulness, that could appear in any Countenance'.[2] Friday is also a model of gratitude, for this, rather than any meaningless contract of obedience, is what makes him such a faithful servant throughout his life.

This belief in gratitude as a 'natural' virtue may be contrasted with Defoe's frequent attacks upon the ingratitude of his age. Pierre Bayle maintained that ingratitude arose when a person was under so great an obligation that he could not hope to repay his debt. Defoe used the same theory in explaining why the English rid themselves of Godolphin and Marlborough, for the nation was '. . . so much in debt to their Services, that they could not be capable of rewarding it, therefore like the corrupted Nature of the whole Race of Man, they hate the Men, . . . because they hate to be in debt beyond the Power of Payment'.[3]

---

[1] *The Evident Approach of a War and Something of the Necessity of it* (1727), p. 40.

[2] *Robinson Crusoe*, ii. 29.

[3] *Atalantis Major* (1711), p. 13. Cf. Bayle, *Dictionary*, ii. 737.

And he complained that this worst violation of the law of nature
had become commonplace in his day:

> Hence Ingratitude, which in its Nature is the Worst of Crimes,
> is the most practised in this Age; and with the more shameless,
> open, avowed Profession of it, than ever it was in any of the more
> ancient Ages of the World. Formerly, to say a Man was Ingrateful
> was to sum up all the Vices which the Nature of Man was capable
> of in one Superlative; but now, to call a Man Ingrate, is laught at as
> an ordinary Thing, worthy of no Notice, meriting no Censure, and,
> in short, a Thing of nothing.[1]

That such a sin was being accepted as the way of the world
seemed to Defoe like an approval of evil itself. 'In a Word', he
concluded, 'when Men have arriv'd to a capacity of acting
Ungratefully to those who have serv'd and oblig'd them; so far
they deviate into Devils, and will afterwards act like Devils
when Opportunity presents.'[2]

Yet gratitude may conflict with other moral principles.
Roxana, for example, is rescued from starvation by her landlord, the jeweller, but after saving her life he asks her to become
his mistress. This gentleman is scrupulous in so far as he
refuses to 'oppress . . . [her] Gratitude' by asking favours of her
under the guise of an obligation.[3] Unfortunately Roxana has
difficulty in distinguishing between gratitude and love. While
she does not exculpate herself entirely, she tries to suggest that
hers was a difficult choice:

> Oh let no Woman slight the Temptation that being generously
> deliver'd from Trouble is to any Spirit furnished with Gratitude and
> just Principles; This gentleman had freely and voluntarily deliver'd
> me from Misery, from Poverty, and Rags; he had made me what I
> was, and put me into a Way to be even more than I ever was, namely
> to live happy and pleas'd and on his Bounty I depended: What could
> I say to this Gentleman when he press'd me to yield to him, and
> argued the Lawfullness of it?[4]

What indeed could Roxana do? Both her fear of future poverty

---

[1] Lee, iii. 345.   [2] Ibid., iii. 349.
[3] *Fortunate Mistress*, i. 36.   [4] Ibid., i. 37.

and her gratitude urge her to accept his love. On the whole, she prefers to plead her case on the basis of necessity, but the force of gratitude is an added palliative. Looking back on her actions, Roxana observes that her gratitude was misplaced, for she should have regarded her landlord as an agent of God and given all her thanks to Him:

> I shou'd have received the Mercy thankfully, and applied it soberly, to the Praise and Honour of my Maker; whereas by this wicked Course, all the Bounty and Kindness of this Gentleman, became a Snare to me, was a meer Bait to the Devil's Hook; I receiv'd his Kindness at the dear Expence of Body and Soul . . . or, if you will, ruin'd my Soul from a Principle of Gratitude, and gave myself up to the Devil, to show myself grateful to my Benefactor.[1]

Never fooled by her landlord's arguments concerning the legality of their 'marriage', she yields from a combination of necessity and gratitude, 'overcome by his Kindness, and terrify'd at the Fear of my own misery if he should leave me'.[2]

In matters of gratitude, as with the problem of necessity, we must separate the penitent's judgement from the facts. At the time, Roxana has no concern with religion. By rewarding a person who has rescued her from death, she is following the laws of nature impeccably. The same cannot be said for her later career, however. For example, she confesses her ingratitude towards the Dutch merchant who saved her life in Paris when she was being threatened by the inquisitive Jew who had become suspicious of her relationship with the murdered landlord. Although she acknowledges her obligation, she refuses to pay her debt. 'It is most certain that, speaking of Originals, I was the Source and Spring of all that Trouble and Vexation to this honest Gentleman', Roxana confesses, 'and as it was afterwards in my Power to have made him full Satisfaction, and did not, I cannot say but I added Ingratitude to all the rest of my Follies.'[3] She thanks him profusely, but, even after she has had a brief affair with him and has become pregnant, refuses to marry him. Roxana regards this affair as an economical way of

[1] Ibid., i. 41.   [2] Ibid., i. 48.   [3] Ibid., i. 156.

cancelling the obligation and never again offers to pay him back for all the money he lost by helping her. She has undergone a change of spirit, and compared with the woman we first see, this ungrateful feminist is indeed one of the 'wickedest Creatures upon Earth'.[1]

Unlike Roxana, Colonel Jack reveals a full sense of gratitude as well as an awareness of the utility of arousing gratitude in others. Sometimes this awareness does not strike us as an admirable quality, for he uses the power of gratitude to break the spirit of Mouchat, a recalcitrant slave, and advances the theory that it is the best means of controlling all slaves. He tells the plantation owner for whom he is working that his method may be practised by anyone:

. . . first to put them into the utmost Horror and Aprehensions of the cruelest Punishment they had ever heard of, and thereby enhance the Value of their Pardon, which was to come as from your self, but not without our great Intercession: Then I was to argue with them, and work upon their Reason, to make the Mercy that was shew'd them sink deep into their Minds, and give lasting Impressions, explain the Meaning of Gratitude to them, and the Nature of an Obligation, and the like, as I had done with *Mouchat*.[2]

Since gratitude is part of the law of nature, the slaves will show a uniform response to such treatment. By nature a kind man, the plantation owner is impressed by Jack's method, agreeing that it would be much better to have his slaves serve him 'from Principles of Gratitude' than from fear.[3]

Jack follows the same theory of gratitude in helping his tutor and in remarrying his ex-wife. After four marriages, he has despaired of finding an honest woman and is willing to accept

---

[1] *Fortunate Mistress*, i. 184. In addition to her other sins against gratitude, chastity, and the law of nature, Roxana indulges in luxury. She even perverts the barbaric Turkish dance which she performs, and by adding 'the *French* Behaviour under the *Mohametan Dress*', succeeds in pleasing the luxurious court far better than the more natural and genuine Armenian maidens who precede her. See *The Fortunate Mistress*, i. 210; and my forthcoming *Economics and the Fiction of Daniel Defoe*, University of California English Studies, ch. 6.

[2] *Colonel Jack*, i. 172.   [3] Ibid., i. 173.

a grateful one. As the arbiter of the Scandal Club, Defoe urged a man to take back his erring wife. 'If this Generosity will not for ever bind her to you in Love and Gratitude', he wrote, 'you will be excused, and she will pass with all honest People for one of the worst of Women.'¹ By placing his trust in the laws of nature and the power of gratitude, Jack is never disillusioned. His tutor proves to be a faithful manager of his estate and his wife a loving and true companion.

II

> Mercy in a Prince is so heavenly a Disposition, that even those who have no need of it for themselves, and have the greatest Aversion to the Crimes which are forgiven, find yet a secret involuntary Pleasure, in seeing other People forgiven.
>
> DEFOE, *A General Pardon Consider'd*²

JACK not only inspires gratitude in others but after King George pardons him for his role in the rebellion of 1715, he is overwhelmed by the generosity of his prince and swears an oath of undying loyalty and gratitude. Defoe had always argued that the Jacobite rebels should be pardoned, for he believed that since they would be living under a constant obligation and 'Duty of Gratitude', they would be the best of citizens. Thus Colonel Jack tells the reader that, like most men of honour, he is ruled by a 'Principle of Gratitude' and proceeds to explain his theory of obligation:

. . . to those who graciously give us our Lives, when it is in their Power to take them away; those Lives are a Debt ever after, and ought to be set a-part for their Service, and Interest, as long as any of the Powers of Life remain; for Gratitude is a Debt that never ceases while the Benefit receiv'd remains; and if my Prince has given me my Life, I can never pay the Debt fully, unless such a Circumstance as this should happen, that the Prince's Life should be in my Power, and I as generously preserv'd it. . . .³

---

¹ *Little Review*, 18b, in *Review*, ii. ² (1717), p. 6.
³ *Colonel Jack*, ii. 114.

But Jack admits that even if he were to save the life of the King, he would not have discharged the debt, since he would be acting from duty to his sovereign, whereas George was acting from magnanimity.

This concept of gratitude as a political force is somewhat different from previous theories we have seen in Defoe, although like Crusoe's insistence on oaths of obedience, it seems to involve a contract. When a ruler pardons a criminal, Jack argues, he does so in the belief that his mercy will create a grateful and obedient subject. If the criminal breaks the law a second time, he forfeits all claim to mercy and merits death. Capital punishment was sometimes considered a violation of the law of nature, but Jack appeals to the '. . . Sketch of the Laws of Honour, printed by the Laws of Nature in the Breast of a Soldier . . .'[1] for his evidence. These laws of gratitude may be seen working in Defoe's Utopian state of Libertalia. Although the citizens have abolished capital punishment, they discover that it must be reinstituted in order to punish two men who have betrayed the state after they had been pardoned once before. Carracioli, the 'Secretary of State', tells the citizens that '. . . he was inclined to the Side of Mercy, till he was thoroughly informed of the Blackness of their Ingratitude . . .', whereupon he concluded that they had committed a kind of suicide and were guilty of their own deaths.[2]

The origin for Jack's arguments may be found in Hobbes's contention that since no one does any act of kindness without expectation of repayment, whether material or spiritual, ingratitude would cause a return to 'the condition of *War*'.[3] By making gratitude into a type of contract, Hobbes changed it into a far more mechanical virtue than it had been before; and La Rochefoucauld later transformed this idea into a succinct maxim. ' 'Tis with Gratitude as with Trust among Tradesmen', wrote the cynical Duke, 'it keeps up Commerce; and we do not pay because 'tis just to discharge our Debts, but to engage

[1] *Colonel Jack*, ii. 115.   [2] *General History of the Pyrates*, ii. 98.
[3] *Leviathan*, p. 101.

People the more easily to lend to us another time.'¹ If we keep
these somewhat disreputable sources in mind, we shall be able
to understand Colonel Jack's concern with gratitude more
clearly. For Jack, gratitude is good because it may be used
advantageously in both public and private life as a dependable
natural virtue, and while he practises it faithfully enough in his
own life, he seems to exploit it for his own purposes in others.

III

> I can neither express or describe the Joy, that touch'd
> my very Soul, when I found, *for it was easy to discover
> that Part*, that he came not as a Stranger, but as a Son to
> a Mother, and indeed a Son, who had never before known
> what a Mother of his own was; in short, we cryed over
> one another a considerable while, when at last he broke
> out first, MY OWN DEAR MOTHER, says he, *are you
> still alive! I never expected to have seen your Face*; as for
> me, I cou'd say nothing a great while.
>
> DEFOE, *Moll Flanders*²

A MORE important theme in Defoe's fiction than gratitude
towards a monarch was the element of obligation which exists
between parents and children and the conflicts which arise
from these obligations. The best example of Defoe's treatment
of this theme may be found in *Robinson Crusoe*. The young
Crusoe has been well cared for by his parents, who have educated him according to their means and are ready to establish
him as an apprentice to a lawyer. Unfortunately his 'Inclination'
is for the sea and travel, and we know that Defoe once advised
fathers to choose a profession such 'as suits the circumstances
we are in, as to their supply, and the inclinations and capacities
of our children'.³ Defoe would certainly have agreed with
Pufendorf's contention that no father has a right 'to compel
Children to a Method of Life, to which their Genius is utterly
averse . . .', but Crusoe's father is perfectly justified in opposing

¹ *Moral Reflections and Maxims* (1706), p. 41.   ² ii. 165.
³ *Serious Reflections*, p. 63.

his son's desire to go to sea.[1] He tells his son that he may choose any other trade he wishes but that God would not bless him if he became a sailor. Crusoe's father may be wrong in refusing to consult his son's inclinations, but his reasons are excellent: he wants his son to lead a comfortable, happy life, and he warns him that the life of a sailor could be both dangerous and miserable. Nevertheless Crusoe violates his obligation to his father, runs away from home to become a sailor and comes to regard this sin against the gratitude which he owed his parents as the 'Original Sin' which brings God's revenge upon him.

The obedience of children, Defoe insisted, while it might be considered a religious duty, was also a law of nature, and through the mask of a Turkish merchant, he complained that in Europe the children often rebel against their mothers and fathers and deviate from and '. . . dishonour even that Nature, whose Dictates they know as well as feel in their own Breasts'.[2] This theme may have been very close to Defoe's heart, for in one of his last letters he accused his son, Daniel, of allowing him to die in poverty and disgrace. But the relationship between children and parents involved mutual obligations as well. Hobbes's contention that there was a contract based on the act of generation which obliged children to absolute obedience was generally considered extreme, and most writers agreed with Pufendorf, who insisted that the obligation arose from gratitude alone. Defoe also agreed, but he believed that this gratitude had to be earned by the parents through their concern for their child's welfare. In the *Serious Reflections* he suggested that, in addition to supporting his family, the father was required to 'discharge his debt' to his children by educating them according to their abilities, by choosing a proper profession for them and by showing them the way to behave in life through his own example.[3] Crusoe's father tries to follow these precepts as well as he can, and all the blame must fall upon the wayward son.

---

[1] *Law of Nature*, p. 121 (VI. ii. 12).

[2] *The Conduct of Christians*, p. 8. See also Defoe's attack on the ingratitude of children towards their parents in *Chickens Feed Capons* (1731), pp. 1-15, 22-24.   [3] p. 63.

Although Defoe dramatized this situation only once in his fiction, his didactic works, such as *The Family Instructor*, are filled with histories of sons who disobeyed their fathers and came to evil ends. In this matter Defoe even felt confident enough to correct the morality of the *Spectator*, which had criticized a stubborn father who had refused to become reconciled with his daughter after she had married against his wishes. Only God, Defoe argued, could be expected to forgive sins against a 'superlative Affection':

Abused Love to return! Insulted Goodness to flow again! A slighted and rejected Tenderness to continue tender! Contemn'd Affections to embrace the Object contemning! This is for God to do—Whose *Mercy is Infinite* above all his Works, and *endures for ever*: But for Men! who are finite! who are but Men!—Govern'd, and indeed Compos'd of Passions and Affections! It cannot be![1]

Thus while the parent may forgive the offence, he may not be able to forgive the offending person. Was Defoe once more thinking of his children and feeling sorry for himself? If so, he still had good grounds, perhaps surer grounds than the Spectator's Christianity, in the laws of nature and the baseness of ingratitude.

But the relationship between children and parents involved mutual obligations as well, and of parents who provide insufficiently for the education of their children, there are ample enough examples in the novels. Defoe's most virulent attack on these neglectful parents appeared in the *Compleat English Gentleman*, where he commiserated with those children who were deprived of an education because their fathers raised them as 'gentlemen'. One of these victims complains that his father '. . . did as other gentlemen do. He took care to leav his son a good estate, and that he thought was enough for a gentleman: my grandfather did the same by him, and my great-grand-father the like, so that we have been a generation of ——'.[2] A few pages later Defoe interrupted his anecdote to comment on these fathers who condemn their sons to ignorance:

[1] *Review*, viii. 331*a*.   [2] *Compleat English Gentleman*, p. 133.

'Tis very hard that it should be in the paternal monarchy what it is not in the national, and that the patriarchal authourity, which, by the way, has been some thousands of yeares abolish'd, should place an absolute power in the head of the house to doom his subjects, that is his children, to be fools or wise men by his meer arbitrary will, and . . . determine arbitrarily, this shall be a schollar, and this a blockhead, or, to speak it in grosser terms, this shall be the wise man, and this a . . . gentleman.[1]

For this 'violence upon Nature' the father was entirely at fault. He has failed to 'discharge his debt' to his child, more specifically, the 'debt of instruction', and in the *Serious Reflections*, Defoe classified such a parent as a 'relative knave'.[2]

Both Moll Flanders and Roxana are partially guilty of the same knavery. Moll seems to give birth to children whom she forgets about entirely, yet she claims that she is not 'unnatural, and regardless of the Safety' of the child she has by her Lancashire husband.[3] After voicing her concern over the fate of this infant, she even indulges in several seemingly inappropriate sermons on natural affection and maternal love:

It is manifest to all that understand any thing of Children, that we are born into the World helpless, and uncapable either to supply our own Wants, or so much as make them known; and that without help, we must Perish; and this help requires not only an assisting Hand, whether of the Mother, or some body else; but there are two Things necessary in that assisting Hand, that is, Care and Skill; without both which, half the Children that are born would die; nay, tho' they were not to be deny'd Food; and one half more of those that remain'd would be Cripples or Fools, loose in their Limbs, and perhaps their Sense.[4]

And she adds that this is the reason why 'Affection was plac'd by Nature in the Hearts of Mothers', for without natural affection, no mother would ever devote herself to the 'Care and waking Pains' which are necessary for raising children.[5]

Moll certainly shows affection for her son Humphry, whom

---

[1] *Compleat English Gentleman*, p. 147.
[2] *Serious Reflections*, p. 62.   [3] *Moll Flanders*, i. 189.
[4] Ibid., i. 185.   [5] Ibid., i. 186.

she sees for the first time in many years. She describes how she is seized by a fit of trembling; her eyes fill with tears, and she kisses the earth where he had been standing. But we may well ask whether these demonstrations of affection are not somewhat inconsistent with her actions. She leaves her children from her first marriage with their grandparents without any apparent regret. Her justification that she has no means of supporting them may seem slight, yet if we consider carefully, it will be apparent that this is a perfectly valid excuse. Pufendorf wrote that the selling or pawning a child was an unnatural act in a parent '. . . except when he cannot otherwise support him. For then he ought rather to sell him into some easy Servitude, whence there is Hope of being releas'd then to let him perish with Hunger'. And quoting Aelian on the rule of delivering a child to the magistrate, he added that 'nature is supposed to give us a Right to every thing, which appears absolutely necessary to our fulfilling her Commands'.[1] Moll has to make her way in the world. When she is settled or is in a condition to appreciate children, she shows the usual natural affection, but when she must find a husband or steal to earn her dinner, she simply cannot concern herself with them.

Roxana presents a different problem. Like Moll, she has to give up her children, albeit reluctantly. 'We had eaten up almost everything', she remarks, 'and little remain'd, unless like one of the pitiful Women of *Jerusalem*, I should eat up my very Children themselves.'[2] She reveals far more affection for these children than Moll for hers, but whereas Moll's heart becomes softer as she grows older, Roxana seems to lose her maternal feeling for her later children, regarding them as a nuisance. Of the baby she has with the prince, she comments somewhat drily that 'after the first Touches of Affection (which are usual, I believe, to all Mothers) were over' she was not sorry that the

---

[1] *Law of Nature*, p. 116 (VI. ii. 9).
[2] *Fortunate Mistress*, i. 16. The story of the 'Women of *Jerusalem*' is probably a reference to an incident during Titus's siege of the city rather than to 2 Kings xxviii. 57. See Josephus, *The Jewish War*, trans. H. St. J. Thackeray (1957), iii. 435–9 (VI. 201–19).

child died.[1] And she calls the infant that she is about to have with the merchant 'the Burthen I had in my Belly'.[2] In spite of these remarks, Roxana is in some ways a kinder mother than Moll. She cares for the merchant's child, although she has no affection for it and uses her ill-gotten wealth for establishing her sons in Italy and the West Indies and for taking her daughters out of servitude in an attempt to reclaim their social position.

Unfortunately Roxana fails her children by not setting a good example for them. Susan, the 'young Slut', guesses that the courtesan for whom she worked and who danced so lasciviously for the dissolute nobility is actually her mother, a discovery which threatens Roxana with the destruction of her marriage to the Dutch merchant and the ruin of her affairs. Susan is unquestionably not the shy, grateful daughter that Roxana might have expected. She has been rescued from the drudgery of servitude too late to have saved her from the impudence and forwardness which Defoe complained was all too universal among the servants in England.

But this is probably the most ambiguous and complex situation in all of Defoe's fiction. Susan is ungrateful for all the favours which Roxana has bestowed on her, yet her desire to see her mother arises, at least partly, from natural affection. Roxana is a bad parent, yet she feels an overwhelming affection for Susan, wants to take her in her arms and hold her, even though she knows that this would lead to discoveries that would destroy her future happiness. Thus Roxana is forced to admit that she 'shou'd have shed but very few Tears' for Susan if she had quietly died of natural causes, and while she refuses to sanction Amy's plan to murder her daughter, she does nothing very definite to prevent Amy from putting her scheme into effect.[3] Critics who have made the mistake of thinking that Defoe was a mere story-teller should consider Roxana's fate more carefully. When the disguised courtesan kisses her daughter, she

---

[1] *Fortunate Mistress*, i. 120.
[2] Ibid., i. 190.   [3] Ibid., ii. 126.

feels an 'Inconceivable Pleasure' and finds it difficult to avoid abandoning herself 'to an Excess of Passion at the first Sight of her'.[1] Cut off from the tender joys of motherhood and almost willing to murder her own daughter, Roxana finds that for all her wealth, she cannot so easily regain the innocent pleasures of life which she has forfeited by her sins.

It is not surprising that the Lilliputians punished ingratitude with death, as a crime against mankind, but, as Swift suggested, this was part of the earlier and more Utopian laws which were no longer in effect. Pufendorf argued that such a law was impractical. Although God would eventually judge and punish those who violated the law of nature, ingratitude was impossible to punish in earthly courts. He dismissed Seneca's contention that unpaid debts of kindness might be turned into real debts, as a violation of the voluntary nature of beneficence and gratitude. We confer a kindness not to have a return of gratitude from fear of compulsion but to have the recipient show his obligation 'out of pure Honesty'. To make a law enforcing gratitude would be to legislate 'Humanity and good Nature' out of existence.[2] Thus Pufendorf concludes with a significant statement concerning crime and punishment in relation to natural law:

. . . from every Transgression of the Law of *Nature*, it does not presently follow that, there must lie an *Action* (or the Resemblance of an *Action*) in *Natures Court*. This is certain, that the Divine Justice hath reserv'd severe Punishments to be inflicted on ungrateful Persons in another Life: And in the present World they ought to suffer the Hatred and Detestation of all Mankind, and to be ajudg'd unworthy of the least Benefit or Favour.[3]

While all crimes against nature 'ought' to be chastised on earth as well as in heaven, this was frequently impossible. But for Defoe, who could play God with his characters, ingratitude was a punishable crime. The Cavalier, obedient and grateful to a

---

[1] Ibid., ii. 96.
[2] *Law of Nature*, p. 199 (III. iv. 18).
[3] Ibid., p. 199 (III. iv. 18).

father who educates and provides for him, leads a life of almost complete happiness, while the ungrateful Crusoe passes twenty-eight years in solitude, lamenting his folly, and Roxana's career ends in 'a dreadful Course of Calamities'.[1]

[1] *Fortunate Mistress*, ii. 160. The relationship between the Cavalier and his father is almost perfect. See *Memoirs of a Cavalier*, Shakespeare Head ed., pp. 1–6, 149–60.

VI

DEFOE'S PSYCHOLOGY AND THE
SEARCH FOR A HERO

There is nothing new, saith Solomon, *under the Sun;*
the same Causes will always produce the same Effects;
and while Mankind bear about them, the various
Passions of Love and Joy, Hatred and Grief, the cunning
Engineer, that stands behind the Curtain, will influence
and work these Passions according to his Malice, to the
destruction of Persons of highest Worth.

DEFOE, *A Short Narrative of the Life and Actions of his
Grace John, D. of Marlborough*[1]

IN this typical generalization about the passions, Defoe considers man as a timeless and immutable abstraction, and as we
have seen, his characters operate in a universe of unchanging
natural law and natural morality. It might be expected that by
following an almost ritualistic pattern of right and wrong,
Defoe's characters run the risk of becoming somewhat patterned
themselves. If this is true, his fiction is not entirely successful,
for we demand of the novelist an ability to create characters
who are not only believable and consistent but also memorable
by their individual differences. I want to suggest in this final
chapter that although Defoe's preoccupation with natural law
enriches the content of his fiction, it also tends to destroy some
of his excellence as a creator of character. Moll, Crusoe, Jack,
and Roxana are all memorable, but frequently their psychology
seems surprisingly uniform. The differences between them
seem to be more a matter of what Ian Watt has described as
'formal realism' than a true realism of character.[2]

This failure to create a realism of character of the kind that
we associate with the novels of Fielding and Richardson was

[1] p. 4. [2] Ian Watt, *The Rise of the Novel* (1957), pp. 32–34.

probably deliberate, since there is no lack of psychological realism in Defoe's didactic works such as the *Family Instructor*, *Religious Courtship*, and *The Great Law of Subordination*. The characters in these works differ from those in the novels in that they seem to be overwhelmed by passions which complicate and intensify their relationships with their families and friends. Here are tales of children who refuse to obey their parents and of parents who cannot control their rage against their children, of fathers who ruin their sons' lives and of children who remain loving and obedient in the face of unreasonable demands by their fathers, of servants who revolt against their masters and of masters who murder their servants in a sudden fit of anger. Nor did Defoe lack a full knowledge of the passions and vices. In the introduction to *Jure Divino* he lamented 'the Wild Anatomy of Sin', which has been the essence of man's soul since the Fall:

> Ambition flows in the degen'rate Seed,
> Pride swells the Heart, and Avarice the Head;
> Envy sits Regent in *the Growing Spleen*,
> And *Hypochondrack Malice* boils within;
> Lust in his *baser Part* obscurely lies,
> And Rage and Passion *sparkle in his Eyes*;
> His *Locomotive Faculties* obey,
> And *Organ* pays Allegiance to the Tyranny;
> The hands obey *the Tyrant in the Brain*,
> Reason *when Lust commands*, resists in vain;
> Unnatural Heats o're all the Blood prevail,
> This Hour they Rule *the Head*, the next *the Tail*;
> With Arbitrary Force the Members guide,
> The *Feet* to Mischief, and the *Hands* to Blood:
> Subjected Man submits to the Controul
> Of Forty thousand Tyrants in his Soul;
> *Alternate Malice* bends his fatal Brow,
> *One Tyrant* Reigns to Day, *to Morrow Two*;
> *Love kills* to Day, to Morrow *Hatred Wounds*,
> *Joy* strikes him dumb, and then *his Grief* confounds;
> Anger to Rage and Madness swells the Breast,
> By abject Patience then as much supprest;

Courage exalts his Soul above his Sphere,
And the next hour *he hangs himself for fear*:
To Day *insults* with High Blaspheming Breath,
To Morrow *strives to Die* for fear of Death.[1]

Now although this list would suggest that Defoe had a fairly complete psychology for the presentation of character, it is apparent that his rendering of passion, at least in his fiction, is not entirely adequate.

Where does the flaw lie? As an example let us compare two sets of passions, joy and love. After Crusoe returns from his island, he discovers that he may reclaim some of the wealth from his plantations in Brazil. He is overwhelmed with joy:

It is impossible to express here the Flutterings of my very Heart, when I look'd over these Letters, and especially when I found all my Wealth about me; for as the *Brasil* Ships come all in Fleets, the same Ships which brought my Letters, brought my Goods; and the Effects were safe in the River before the Letter came to my Hand. In a Word, I turned pale, and grew sick; and had not the old Man run and fetch'd me a Cordial, I believe the sudden Surprize of Joy had overset Nature, and I had dy'd upon the Spot.[2]

A similar scene depicting the change from grief to joy occurs when Moll Flanders hears of her reprieve from death. She faints from happiness '. . . for as grief had overset me before, so Joy overset me now . . .', and she explains that 'the Passions on such Occasions as these, are certainly so agitated as not to be able to presently regulate their own Motions'.[3] Other examples of this kind of reaction are Colonel Jack's 'Flood of Joy' when he rediscovers his lost money and Crusoe's emotion when he realizes that he is to be rescued.[4] For Defoe, passion was a movement of animal spirits which may fall into 'Confusion and Amazement' when the motion is too sudden.[5] There is nothing very original in this theory, nor is it difficult to translate it into modern terms. The trouble is that all the emotional responses

---

[1] p. iv.   [2] *Robinson Crusoe*, ii. 81.
[3] *Moll Flanders*, ii. 117, 118.
[4] See *Colonel Jack*, i. 29; and *Robinson Crusoe*, ii. 68.
[5] See Charron, *Of Wisdom*, i. 169 (i. xviii. 2); and *King Lear*, v. iii. 195–9.

are exactly the same, that Defoe was delineating an emotion divorced from the person experiencing it.

In the same manner, both Roxana and Moll have the same emotional response to the sight of their children on seeing them after the lapse of many years, and Moll suggests that her feelings are the same as those of any mother in the same circumstances:

. . . let any Mother of Children that reads this, consider it, and but think with what anguish of Mind I restrain'd myself; what yearning of Soul I had in me to embrace him, and weep over him; and how I thought all my Entrails turn'd within me, that my very Bowels mov'd, and I knew not what to do; as I now know not how to express those Agonies: When he went from me I stood gazing and trembling, and looking after him as long as I could see him; then sitting down on the Grass, just at a Place I had mark'd, I made as if I lay down to rest me, but turn'd from her, and lying on my Face wept, and kiss'd the Ground that he had set his Foot on.[1]

After kissing her daughter, from whom she must hide her identity, Roxana experiences the same violent sensation:

No pen can describe, no Words can express, I say, the strange Impression which this thing made upon my Spirits; I felt something shoot thro' my Blood; my Heart flutter'd,,; my Head flash'd and was dizzy, and all within me, *as I thought*, turn'd about, and much ado I had, not to abandon myself to an Excess of Passion at the first Sight of her, much more when my Lips touch'd her Face; I thought I must have taken her into my Arms, and kiss'd her again a thousand times, whether I wou'd or no.[2]

At first it might seem that the major objection to these scenes is that previously neither Moll nor Roxana has evinced any strong emotions towards her children. But Moll has a certain streak of sentimentality in her, and Roxana might be expected to show some emotion at the sight of a daughter who belonged to a part of her life which was comfortable and respectable. The real difficulty is that their reactions are merely the 'natural' emotions of any woman in these circumstances, not specifically

---

[1] *Moll Flanders*, ii. 152.   [2] *Fortunate Mistress*, ii. 96.

those of Moll or Roxana. Defoe has failed to delineate the entire character, and we do not see Moll's love for her son but love itself. Defoe was proud of his realistic description of the maid's hunger in the *Farther Adventures*, but the hunger which she experiences is a general sensation having nothing to do with her personality.[1]

This is certainly one of his major defects as a novelist, and it was a fault which his approach to fiction through natural law encouraged. Although his characters are very different, they tend towards a single general type in their emotions. Instead of the blend of reason, passion, self-love, sympathy, benevolence, and a moral sense, which was to become the basic psychology of the English novel, Defoe presented a set of characters ruled by reason and self-love alone, except when they were moved by individual passions. And frequently a passion appears to be grafted on to the characters, an appendage rather than an organic part of them.

This deficiency, however, is not as damaging as it might first appear. '. . . a *Coldness of the Passions* is, as it were, the Natural Principle of Prudence and Probity amongst Men', wrote Pufendorf, whose distrust of the passions and admiration for the reason was typical of almost all writers on natural law.[2] They acknowledged that men differed according to climate, soil, diet, and age but never felt that any of these differences

---

[1] Some defence might be made for Defoe by comparing these scenes with the tragedy of the period, in which passion is seldom integrated with the personalities of the characters. Indeed it is very likely that Defoe's interest in the theatre, which seems to have begun in 1715, influenced his writing of these scenes. But what is acceptable in tragedy may not be so in the novel. A large part of Defoe's excellence as a novelist rests in his insight into human nature, and a dramatic rendering of passion is not sufficient in a form allowing for more analysis. Fielding may be charged with the same defect, especially in *Joseph Andrews*, but he defends himself by stating emphatically, 'I describe not men but manners; not an individual, but a species. See Henry Fielding, *Works*, ed. William Henley (1902), i. 215. For Defoe's interest in the theatre see John Robert Moore, *Defoe* (1958), pp. 25–26. Defoe wrote one act of a play into his pamphlet *The Candidate* (1715), pp. 42–57, and contemplated writing the first volume of *The Family Instructor* as a 'dramatic poem'.

[2] *Law of Nature*, p. 131 (II. vi. 12).

could be strong enough to incline the will irresistibly away from rational action. Thus Defoe believed that Peter the Wild Boy might become the ideal man—the man above passion. As an animal, he admitted, Peter was not exceptional:

> But speaking of a human Species, the Case alters, and there, I confess, to act as a Man, and to have no Pride, no Ambition, no Avarice, no Rancour or Malice, no ungovern'd Passion, no unbounded Desires, how infinitely more happy is he than Thousands of his more inform'd and better-taught Fellow Brutes in human Shape, who are every Day raging with Envy gnawing their own Flesh, that they are not rich, great, and cloath'd with Honours and Places as such-and-such, studying to supplant, suppress, remove, and displace those above them, and even to slander, accuse, murder and destroy to get into their Places? Had Nature been beneficent to him, in bestowing something more upon him other ways, and yet kept his Soul lock'd up as to these Things, how had he been the happiest of all the Race of Rationals in the World?[1]

Man's dilemma is that he cannot know good without knowing evil, and to give Peter knowledge of virtue alone would be impossible.

Defoe leaves no doubt in the reader's mind, however, that Peter would benefit by tasting of the tree of knowledge. 'Reason is the Gift that distinguishes Men from the Brutes;' he wrote, 'and 'tis observable that where a Man is depriv'd of the Use of his Reason, the sensitive Life that remains in him is less sagacious than in the Common Brutes; he's much more helpless and despicable, and . . . makes the meanest sort of Beast. . . .'[2] This emphasis on reason may seem typical of the age, but even Pufendorf believed that man must come to terms with his passions. Rochester's warning that man should rely on 'modest sense' and Locke's doubts about the limits of reason were far more representative of contemporary opinion. Just as Peter is not extraordinary when considered as a brute, so Swift did not think it at all strange in his Utopia that a race of rationals might exist, but he refused to portray them as human beings: rational horses, perhaps, but not rational men. Fixed in the

---

[1] *Mere Nature Delineated*, p. 43.
[2] *Jure Divino*, bk. iii, p. 5.

scale of being as a creature of passions as well as reason, man's best chance of obtaining happiness was to know himself and make some compromise with his limitations.

For almost two centuries a large number of treatises on human nature attempted to reconcile man's faculties, first his passions, understanding, and will, and later, his self-love, benevolence, and moral sense. Since the passions seemed to be the weakness in man's nature, most writers tried to justify them as part of God's plan. In the seventeenth century the usual position was Aristotelian: the passions were considered as a part of man's nature which, if kept under the control of reason and religious principles, would lead him to virtue. By the eighteenth century they were extolled as excellent in themselves. 'Reason', wrote Isaac Watts, 'is too often called away from a due Attention to a present necessary Idea by many sensible Objects . . . too slow and too weak to excite a sudden and vigorous Activity in many Cases; but Passion is sudden and strong for this Purpose.'[1] From Watts's arguments it was not too far to those of David Hume, who contended that 'Reason is, and ought only to be, the slave of the passions, and can never pretend to any other office than to serve and obey them'.[2] In other words the eighteenth century, in its optimistic effort to demonstrate that all was for the best, eventually came to view the passions as the better part of man. Certain that the passions could never lead man astray, the school of sentiment began to insist that passion was far more appealing than the 'Coldness' which Pufendorf praised. For all his imprudence, it is Tom Jones whom we admire, not the self-interested Blifil.

But Defoe's ideas on the passions seem, at times, to resemble those of an extreme school of thought which regarded passion as the chief obstacle to human aspiration. *Man without Passion: or the Wise Stoick* by Antoine Le Grand indicates by its title that the theory of a life divorced from emotion and vice had its

---

[1] *The Doctrine of the Passions Explain'd and Improv'd*, 2nd ed. (1732), p. 82.
[2] *Treatise of Human Nature*, ed. L. A. Selby-Bigge (1888), p. 415 (II. iii. 3).

origins in the revival of stoicism. 'Reason', wrote Le Grand, 'is . . . Man's only benefit: he must use it to climbe Heaven, he must consult it to govern his Life, and if he do but hearken unto her, he shall be vertuous, and tame the most insolent of his *Passions*.'[1] Defoe expressed a similar theory in the *Review*, after a poem praising the man who could attain happiness by keeping '*his rising Passions at a full Command*'.[2] 'Were the Mind once arriv'd to so Sublime a State', he philosophized, 'as to be unmoved with the various Changes of this Life, how uninterrupted might the Happiness of Mankind be?' If the passions could be removed entirely, all might be well:

What Evils do Men undergo, by the Slavery they are in to their Passions? I have not more Contemptible Thoughts of a Dog, a Bear, or any Brute, than I have of a Man, whom I see easie to be *provok'd*, or soon *dejected*; those two Things render a Man perfectly uncapable of Managing himself, either in Prosperity or Adversity: In the first he runs out to all the Excesses of a Tyrant, and commits the most Extravagant Things in the World: In the last, he is the most Soul-less, dispirited Thing in the World, and is fit for nothing but to despair, and perhaps, at last, die for fear of Death.

On the contrary, the 'true Heroe' is able to show 'Moderation, Patience, and a due Restraint of the Mind' in either prosperity or adversity.[3]

When we consider these statements on the passions, it is not surprising that Defoe's delineation of emotion tended to be mechanical. But just as Pufendorf put off a thorough discussion of the passions because he was more concerned with problems of law and morality, so Defoe may be said to have done the same in his novels. His major concern was moral rather than psychological, and when he used pride, avarice, ambition, fear, and courage in his fiction, he regarded these qualities less as passions than as virtues and vices which might be evaluated on the basis of how much happiness or unhappiness they produced in mankind. In such a scheme, the passionate man is a fool, and when

---

[1] Trans. G. R. (1675), p. 27.   [2] *Review*, viii. 721.
[3] Ibid., viii. 722a.

we turn to the qualities which Defoe admired in the 'true Heroe', we will see that not the least of these was his ability to rule his passions.

II

A Finish'd Hero does not grow up every Day, they are scarce Plants and do not thrive in every Soil; He may be easily lost, but then that Loss cannot easily be repair'd; therefore there is great Reason to Value and Esteem him.

DEFOE, *A Short Narrative of the Life of Marlborough*[1]

CARLYLE would have recognized Defoe as a typical hero-worshipper, and Defoe would have been the last to deny it. He once remarked that he never tried to 'feign a Hero'.[2] He often praised his patron, Harley, yet at no time does he confuse the qualities of the Treasurer with those of a hero. One might suppose that this was because he conceived of heroism in strictly military terms, but among his heroes are statesmen and explorers as well as kings and generals. The select list includes men whom Defoe admired without reservation and those for whom admiration is tempered by dislike. Only Gustavus Adolphus and William III seem to have won Defoe's entire approbation, although, in spite of certain reservations, he acknowledged the greatness of Marlborough, Sir Walter Raleigh, Fairfax, Richelieu, Peter the Great, and Charles XII.

What are the qualities of these heroes? In describing Marlborough as his 'Finish'd Hero', Defoe remarked that he was 'Temperate, Sober, Careful, Couragious, Politick, Skilful, . . . Courteous, Mild, Affable, Humble, and Condescending to People of the meanest Condition'.[3] Although he was later to revise his estimate of Marlborough somewhat, Defoe praised him for pursuing 'true Vertue for its own Reward'.[4] These are also the qualities of Fairfax, whose greatness wins the admiration

---

[1] p. 45.   [2] 'The Double Welcome', in *A True Collection*, ii. 170.
[3] *A Short Narrative of the Life of Marlborough*, p. 45.
[4] 'The Double Welcome', in *A True Collection*, ii. 172.

of Defoe's Cavalier even though they are fighting on opposing sides. The central virtue of Fairfax and Marlborough is courage, and it is courage which qualifies Charles XII as a hero even though he ruined his own nation through his interminable wars. This virtue alone will make a man heroic, and Defoe was un-questionably in complete agreement with his narrator's descrip-tion of Charles as a 'true Heroe' in *The History of the Wars of Charles XII.*[1] Defoe did not pardon his folly and recklessness, but when Charles died, Defoe wrote an elegy which described him in terms which he used only for William and Gustavus.[2]

'Courage', Defoe maintained, 'is, if not the Source, at least the sign of all the vertues, in Princes, especially.'[3] Since Defoe seems to have agreed with Rochester's contention that fear was the source of almost all human action, it is not surprising that he should have regarded courage, a seeming defiance of man's natural state, as the central virtue. He called it 'the most funda-mental Part of Morality', for the virtues of a coward could not be considered permanent.[4] But because courage was a passion, it might be used for evil as well as good. 'So Courage', he wrote, '(in it self highly Valuable) happening to be join'd with Strength, in Men of *selfish, violent,* and *unjust* Tempers; hurries them on to all kinds of Wickedness, and makes them but the more dangerous to Societies.'[5] Although Defoe occasionally tried to distinguish between a virtuous courage (fortitude) and that type which he described as 'a kind of Sin of stupidity', he seems to have been equally fascinated by the courage of the soldier and the courage of the criminal.

In *An Apology for the Army,* which contains his fullest dis-

---

[1] (1720), p. 386.
[2] See *Mercurius Politicus* (January 1719), p. 14:
  From Age to Age they shall be handed on,
  From th' Knowing Father, to th' Enquiring Son;
  Till *Fable takes it,* and it Grows so Great,
  Their *Sons, Sons, Sons,* shall ask *what Gyant's That?*
Cf. 'The Mock Mourners' in *A True Collection,* i. 60.
[3] *The Englishman's Choice* (1694), p. 21.
[4] *A Collection of Miscellany Letters* (1722), ii. 37.
[5] *An Apology for the Army* (1715), p. 14.

cussion of fortitude, he divided his subject into three categories: a 'Courage of Constitution', a 'Courage of Reason', and a 'Courage of Honour'. The courage of constitution, or physical courage, needs little explanation, but the courage of reason is important for our purposes, for this is the bravery of those in necessity who display a 'Resolution foreign from their Tempers'.[1] Only the courage of honour, however, reveals what Defoe referred to as *true* Magnanimity'. 'What they call true courage', he remarked in the *Family Instructor*, 'consists in sustaining the mind under the most pressing afflictions, and passive valour is the greatest extreme of true magnanimity; whereas he that destroys himself is a coward, and dies for fear of the bitterness of life.'[2] Thus while Defoe praised the bravery of the Swedes when they were actively fighting under the banner of Charles XII, he admired their passive courage even more:

. . . *Swedish* Courage is as great as ever it was; nay, greater, tho' in a different Kind; for as before they were actively courageous even beyond Reason; so now, which is a much greater Thing, they can be cooly and passively brave; and bear being attack'd with Caution and Circumspection.[3]

The essence of passive courage, then, is patience in the midst of suffering, and when the fortunes of politics had driven him into an untenable position, for lack of a better answer to his enemies, Defoe would pose as the patient, innocent Job, the epitome of passive courage.

Although Defoe's definition of courage might apply to the problems of private life as well as war, his truly great heroes, William and Gustavus, were men of active courage in the field as well as statesmen fighting in the cause of justice and truth. As we have seen, the statesman may be a hero if he can display four qualities: '*CAPACITY, INTEGRITY, COURAGE*, and *APPLICATION*.'[4] Capacity includes all the heroic leader's

[1] Ibid., p. 15.
[2] Tegg ed., xv. 381. See also Defoe, *Memoirs of Captain Carleton*, ed. Cyril Hartman (1929), p. 19.
[3] *Mercurius Politicus* (July 1720), p. 11.
[4] *Rogues on Both Sides*, p. 30. See above, p. 59.

virtues and abilities, his justness, intelligence, learning, constancy, and modesty. 'It absolutely excludes Pride', the worst of all vices in a hero. By integrity Defoe meant the political hero's adherence to religious principles and his sacrifice of his own interest to that of the public; by his courage, he meant the *'Resolution*, to despise Danger and support with Constancy any Evil . . .'. Such a courage is always supported by wisdom and 'right Reason'. Of the final virtue, application, Defoe merely distinguished it from 'a perpetual *drudging* at the *Oar'*, since it included both inventiveness and originality.[1]

The model for all of these qualities was William, his hero-king, a man entirely free from pride, fear, and the desire for power:

> *My Hero, with the Sails of Honour Furl'd,*
> *Rises like the Great Genius of the World.*
> *By Fate and Fame wisely prepar'd to be*
> The Soul of War, and Life of Victory.[2]

William's name, he remarked, should never be mentioned without the 'Addition of *Great, Immortal, Glorious, Wise, Just, Penetrating'*.[3] To such a leader all the liberties of the subject and the power of the state might be entrusted not only without fear but with a certainty that both the state and its citizens would share some of this leader's greatness. Such an ideal hero must be kept in mind when we consider the protagonists of Defoe's fiction.

---

[1] *Rogues on Both Sides*, pp. 30–33.

[2] 'The True Born Englishman' in *The Shortest Way with the Dissenters*, p. 61.

[3] *An Argument Proving that the Design of Employing and Enobling Foreigners, Is a Treasonable Conspiracy* (1717), p. 58.

III

Nor had Death been the Punishment Should I have been
So Long before I had Come in and Thrown my Self upon
her Majties Clemency, but Jayls, Pillorys and Such like
with which I have been So Much Threatn'd have Con-
vinc't me I want Passive Courage, and I Shall Never for
the Future Think my Self Injur'd if I am Call'd a Coward.

DEFOE, *Letters*[1]

FEW of Defoe's letters contain any kind of self-analysis, but in
these remarks to Paterson, written while he was in prison, Defoe
seems to have been searching his soul with a good deal of perception. His confession to a lack of passive courage, the quality
which he admired most of all, reveals his acute awareness of
a separation between the hero and the ordinary man, between
the heroic and the commonplace. Are we then to suppose that
Defoe regarded the narrators of his novels as heroes or that he
confused their cunning with wisdom and their ability to survive
with 'true magnanimity'? Since all of Defoe's narrators undergo
a trial of courage, this virtue is a good means of comparing their
inherent worth.

The most obviously courageous figure in Defoe's fiction is
the Cavalier, although his modesty precludes more than a few
examples of his bravery. Educated at Oxford as a gentleman,
interested in history, geography, and travel, he is indeed Defoe's
ideal gentleman. He fights without pay for the Protestant cause
in the service of Gustavus Adophus and later for King Charles
in the wars against Scotland and the Parliament. The Cavalier
is humble, honest, and disinterested and has that kind of
courage which seldom appears in Defoe's other characters, the
courage of honour. He is not entirely without fear and flees the
plague in Italy with the admission that he had 'no manner of
Courage for that Risque', but when there is a possibility of
victory, the Cavalier stands his ground.[2]

The fair-minded Cavalier fits Defoe's idea of a hero perfectly,
yet he is hardly more than a narrative device for a description

[1] p. 6.   [2] *Memoirs of a Cavalier*, p. 26.

of the religious wars of the seventeenth century. Here there is no irony, little satire, and not very much pious exhortation or beating of the breast over sins. Unlike Crusoe, the Cavalier's relations with his parents are excellent, and in his one encounter with a prostitute he reveals an embarrassment and horror at sexual licence. In commenting on the religious disputes between the forces of Charles and the Parliament, he confesses that he was not concerned with the technical aspects of the spiritual controversies of the age and not very much interested in religion in general:

For my part, I confess I had not much Religion in me, at that time; but I thought Religion rightly practised on both Sides would have made us all better Friends; and therefore sometimes I began to think, that both the Bishops of our Side, and the Preachers on theirs, made Religion rather *the Pretence* than *the Cause* of the War.[1]

Here then is a character who might serve as a conventional hero. Why then did not Defoe choose such types more often for his central characters.

The answer is that the Cavalier belongs in the tradition of the 'memoir' as Defoe borrowed it from such works as the *Mémoires de le Comte de Rochefort* by Gatien de Courtilz in which the narrator remains a shadowy figure next to Richelieu or Mazarin.[2] A novel like *Colonel Jack* also borrows much from this genre, but something is added—a realism of scene and complexity of character which was already available to Defoe as a literary technique in the criminal biography. Like the Cavalier, Jack possesses the courage of honour, but it is a quality which Jack has to learn in his effort to become a gentleman. We have some doubts about his courage at first, for after he refuses to fight a duel with his wife's lover, Jack also has doubts. His confession of being 'frighted to the last Degree' shows that he lacks the thoughtless courage of constitution, but when the lover calls him a coward, Jack, now a 'Coward made desperate', throws him to the ground.[3]

---

[1] *Memoirs of a Cavalier*, p. 185.
[2] For a brief discussion of the influence of this work on Defoe see John Robert Moore, *Daniel Defoe* (1958), p. 246.   [3] *Colonel Jack*, ii. 22.

As we discover later, this episode gives little indication that Jack is a coward. He merely refuses to fight a battle which he has no chance of winning and which, at the time, he does not perceive as a challenge to his honour. Jack's natural reactions reflect Defoe's attack on the laws of duelling as an invention of the Devil and his special objection to fighting over an unfaithful wife. '. . . if a Man has so affronted or offended me, that I think he ought to dye for it', wrote Defoe, 'where is the Sence of my laying him an even Wager, whether he shall have his Throat cut that has offered me an Injury, or I that have receiv'd it?'[1] And Defoe followed this statement with a story about a man who, after discovering his wife's adultery, dismissed her from his house and refused to fight a duel. By Defoe's standards, this man was not a coward and neither was Colonel Jack. Even if his opponent had given him a sword, since he had forgotten to include fencing among his newly learned accomplishments, he would have had no opportunity of winning; it would have been merely a 'Private Murther' rather than an affair of honour.[2] After leaving England, Jack enlists as a soldier in Italy and proves to his own satisfaction that he is not a coward:

. . . had he attack'd me now, tho' in the very same Condition, I should, naked and unarm'd as I was, have flewn in the Face of him, and trampl'd him under my Feet; but Men never know themselves till they are tried, and Courage is acquir'd by Time and Experience of Things.[3]

For his bravery, he is made a Lieutenant-Colonel, but Jack is not the generous soldier that the Cavalier is. Although he may have absorbed some of the ideals of honour connected with his new profession, he has not rid himself entirely of the ideals of a plantation owner. His thoughts are still centred on his 'Effects' and on those military adventures which increased his wealth. Nevertheless his behaviour towards his second adulterous wife is impeccable by Defoe's standards. He demurs about fighting a duel, but when his wife's gallant insists, meets the challenge and wins easily.

[1] *Review*, i. 79a.   [2] Ibid., i. 90a.   [3] *Colonel Jack*, ii. 29.

Jack may be said to combine two kinds of courage: the courage of honour, which he learns, and the courage of reason, which he displayed throughout his youth as a pickpocket in London and an indentured servant in America. Defoe defined the courage of reason as the resolution shown 'when People by Nature timerous are urged by Necessity' to survive by whatever means they can discover.[1] All of Defoe's heroes have this kind of courage, for it is merely a refusal to yield to despair. I have quoted before Defoe's somewhat obscure remark that the man who will not leave the ditch will die in the ditch. The story to which he was referring was from Roger L'Estrange's collection of fables:

A *Carter* that had laid his Wagon Fast in a Slough, stood Gaping and Bawling to as many of the Gods and Goddesses as he could Muster up, and to *Hercules* Especially, to Help him out of the Mire. Why ye Lazy Puppy you, says *Hercules*, lay your Shoulder to the Wheel, and Prick your Oxen first, and *Then's* your Time to Pray. Are the Gods to do your Drudgery, d'ye think, and you lie Bellowing with Your Finger in your Mouth?[2]

L'Estrange drew two morals: that '*Hercules* helps no Body that will not help *Himself*' and that prayer without action is frequently ostentatious.[3] It is not at all strange that Defoe should have utilized two ideas so associated with what we think of as the 'Protestant ethic', but his preference for a secular rather than a biblical source is a good indication of his reliance on natural morality rather than religion.

Even Crusoe, who is not a man of outstanding constitutional courage, refuses to lie in the ditch when necessity forces him to act. Although the fear which Crusoe showed on the island was exactly what might have been expected of natural man in such circumstances, it should be noted that he shows little courage elsewhere. When he has made the mistake of buying a ship

[1] *An Apology for the Army*, p. 15.
[2] *Fables of Aesop* (1704), i. 221. Cf. above, p. 84, and *Mercurius Politicus* (October 1720), p. 54.
[3] Ibid., i. 221–2.

formerly owned by pirates and is being pursued along the coast
of south-east Asia, Crusoe falls into a panic. He tells the reader
how, moved by 'that blind useless Passion' fear, he found his
imagination conjuring up all the terrifying things that might
happen if the vessel were captured:

. . . indeed I must acknowledge, that of all the Circumstances of
Life that ever I had any Experience of, nothing makes Mankind so
compleatly miserable, as that, of being in constant Fear: Well does
the Scripture say, *the Fear of Man brings a Snare*; it is a Life of
Death, and the Mind is so entirely suppress'd by it, that it is capable of no Relief; the animal Spirits sink, and all the Vigour of nature,
which usually supports Men under other Afflictions, and is present
to them in the greatest Exigencies, fails them here.[1]

Although occasionally some of his 'Natural Courage' would
show itself, and he would picture himself fighting bravely with
imaginary enemies, Crusoe admits that he does not have an
immoderate amount of physical courage. Yet he never despairs
for long, and through his religious faith he is able to conquer
his irrational fears. Divine grace is important in helping Crusoe
to quell his passions, but long before he becomes resigned to
God's goodness in saving his life by casting him on his island,
Crusoe takes the initial steps of rescuing his equipment from
the wreck and trying to discover a safe habitation. What grace
adds to this refusal to despair is a passive courage, which enables
the restless Crusoe to submit to his fate without murmuring
against the injustice of Providence.

   It may be said then, that in spite of Defoe's attempt to distinguish between types of courage, he admired even Crusoe's
half-hearted bravery. Courage gives to his characters an heroic
stature, which, combined with capacity and a truly inventive
kind of application, enables Singleton, Moll, and Roxana to
attain the heights of their respective professions. Singleton is the
hero as pirate, Moll the heroine as queen of the underworld, and
Roxana as queen of the *demi-monde*. Although lacking in what
Defoe would have called 'integrity', they are heroes in a minor

---

[1] *Robinson Crusoe*, iii. 138–9.

key. Singleton, for example, like most of the pirates who people the pages of Defoe's biographies of real pirates, is a man of constitutional courage, that kind which may be found in both villains and heroes. But Defoe did not necessarily classify the pirate as a villain, for he knew that the best and bravest seamen turned to piracy when they could not find work. Pirates like Edward Low combined a natural bravery with an almost insane cruelty, yet Defoe regarded even this vicious kind of courage as worthy of study. '*It is Bravery and Strategem in War which make Actions worthy of Record*', he argued, '*in which Sense the Adventures here related will be thought deserving that Name.*'[1] And the fictional character who comes closest to approximating Defoe's heroic ideal is the brave, just, visionary pirate, Captain Misson.

Yet Misson is the exception to the rule. Defoe's admiration for courage was somewhat indiscriminate, and, in some ways, he found the courage of good men less interesting than that of the wicked:

A wise Man, and a Truly brave Man, writes *Nil desperandum* upon everything that is before him; he gives up no Cause that ought to be Defended, while there is the least Room to defend it. To abandon his Cause and his Country is the worst of Despair; and Despair is the Extreme of Cowardice and Fear.[2]

But while the courage of the wise man and the Christian is 'sublime', that of the wicked is more amazing:

Here is another kind of Courage exerted, which, though in the particular Circumstances of it, is detestable, yet, in its Nature, is a wonderful Thing; and how human Nature can be brought up to such a height of Courage is hard to describe.[3]

Such a man fights not only against his fellow creatures but against God as well and brings upon himself an everlasting punishment.

This preoccupation with the courage of evil men can be seen most clearly in Defoe's treatment of Captain Singleton, who may be described as a brave man entirely in the service of the

[1] *General History of the Pyrates*, i. sig. A4.   [2] Lee, iii. 298.
[3] Ibid., iii. 300.

Devil. He refuses to discuss his cruelties, which he tells the
reader are best left buried in silence, and limits himself to a
description of his adventures. His courage is such a dominant
part of his character that he will fight merely for physical
enjoyment. The practical William Walters has to remind him
that his main task is to take booty in as efficient a manner as
possible, but in actuality this is not his main concern. The
pattern of respectable work and retirement which William per-
suades Singleton to accept belongs entirely to the creed of a
renegade Quaker. Singleton's real interest is in adventure and
battle, and, in the final analysis, it is not very clear how different
he is from the honourable Cavalier. Singleton's courage may be
entirely constitutional, but there can be no doubt that Defoe
presents this most successful of all pirates as a worthy and
enterprising young man. This is partly because of Singleton's
position as a narrator, yet even in those criminal biographies
where Defoe claims to make moral distinctions, Jack Shepperd
assumes almost heroic dimensions beside the cowardly, cruel
thief Le Febvre.

This same kind of constitutional courage appears in the
characters of Moll Flanders and her Lancashire husband, both
of whom write *Nil desperandum* on every adventure in life.
Theirs is a rational courage based on a constitutional toughness
which Defoe probably associated with the lower classes, since
it is not discoverable in either Roxana or Crusoe. Defoe once
asked his readers whether courage was a habit or a quality,
confessing that he believed it to be both. Certainly Moll
becomes increasingly daring as she discovers her natural abilities as a thief and eventually announces proudly that she was
the 'greatest artist' of her age. But the basis of her hardened
courage is rational and physical.

Even when she is in prison, where her courage is tested by
the prospect of what seems like a certain and ignominious
death, Moll refuses to despair. Initially terrified by Newgate,
she gradually accommodates herself to the desperate gaiety—
a gaiety which she had found so wearisome as a young woman

when she encountered it in the Mint, the debtor's sanctuary. The philosophy of the condemned prisoners is expressed by one of the women who has been living under a suspended death for four months:

I can't help myself, what signifyes being sad? If I am hang'd there's an End of me, and away she turn'd Dancing, and Sings as she goes, the following Piece of *Newgate* Wit,

If I swing by the String,
I shall hear the Bell ring,
And then there's an End of poor Jenny.[1]

Swift's irony concerning 'clever *Tom Clinch*, who hung like a Hero, and never would flinch' was far more typical of the social attitudes of the Augustan age than Defoe's admiration for the courage of the highwayman.[2] Yet Defoe was doubtful if the behaviour of Moll's Newgate companion could be described as courage. Moll, herself, soon discovers that this 'Hell' could become 'not only tollerable, but even agreeable', and it is only when she begins to repent that she again experiences fear.[3]

This new terror, however, is not to be confused with the 'useless Passion' which seized Crusoe, for to pretend a carelessness in circumstances where death seems inevitable is too much for the courage of reason. Moll's repentance originates in her 'fear of Death', but he who is fearless in such a situation is not ruled by courage but by a dullness of mind. The sight of her Lancashire husband in prison restores Moll's sense of guilt and fear and with them her awareness of her present condition and her past life. 'In short', she says, 'I began to think, and to think indeed is one real Advance from Hell to Heaven; all that harden'd State and Temper of Soul, which I said so much of before, is but a Deprivation of Thought; he that is restored to his Thinking, is restor'd to himself.'[4] Moll's growing sense of fear, therefore, is an indication of a new self-knowledge, and like Singleton, who feels terror for the first time when he begins

---

[1] *Moll Flanders*, ii. 100.
[2] *Poems*, ed. Harold Williams (1958), ii. 400.
[3] *Moll Flanders*, ii. 101.   [4] Ibid., ii. 107.

to repent, she learns that the fear of God is not cowardice but wisdom.

That Moll has not lost her courage is evident at her trial, where she bravely refuses to faint when the death sentence is read and even manages to address the judges. 'I spoke with more Courage than I thought I cou'd have done . . .', she remarks, and her tears almost move the court to mercy.[1] Only when death seems unavoidable does Moll begin to despair, but with the news of the reprieve her spirits rebound at once. Thus Moll's spirits are virtually indomitable. She has no dread of being transported to America; her faith that she can begin her life again has the air of eternal youth.

Perhaps even more courageous than Moll is the saddler in the *Journal of the Plague Year*, for his is a courage proceeding entirely from divine grace. Living in the midst of death, despair, and disease, he is sustained by his conviction that God has chosen him to remain in the stricken city. This 'sublime Courage' is unique among Defoe's narrators; Crusoe, for all his former religious devotions, assuages his terror of the cannibals not by prayer but by strengthening the fortifications of his castle. The saddler, on the contrary, decides that if it is God's will, he has no choice but to remain in London during the plague, since to leave would be 'a kind of flying from God'.[2] At times he repents his decision, and he attacks the folly of those who remained without a specific calling:

Upon the foot of all these Observations, I must say, that tho' Providence seem'd to direct my Conduct to be otherwise; yet it is my Opinion, and I must leave it as a Prescription, (*viz.*) *that the best Physick against the Plague is to run away from it.* I know People encourage themselves, by saying, God is able to keep us in the midst of Danger, and able to overtake us when we think our selves out of Danger; and this kept Thousands in the Town, whose Carcasses went into the Great Pits by Cart Loads; and who, if they had fled from the Danger, had, I believe, been safe from Disaster; at least 'tis probable they had been safe.[3]

[1] Ibid., ii. 112.   [2] *Journal of the Plague Year*, p. 12.
[3] Ibid., p. 240.

The saddler suggests that courage in such a situation is a matter of individual belief. Since the plague was ultimately a product of God's will, neither a courage of reason nor of honour could sustain the mind. To remain was not like fighting a battle, '. . . it was charging Death it self on his pale Horse; to stay was indeed to die, and it could be esteemed nothing less. . . .'[1]

And he concludes that the courage shown by those who remained was neither a test of true virtue nor of religious faith. Those who boasted of their bravery lacked an understanding of the nature of man, and he asks whether many of these men '. . . do not sometimes owe their Courage to their Ignorance, and despising the Hand of their Maker, which is a criminal kind of Desperation, and not a true Courage'.[2] Was the 'brutal Courage' of the poor, who did not have the means to leave, greater than that of the saddler's brother who fled? The answer is that all courage must be evaluated according to honour and reason, and neither is tested in a battle against the plague. The brave Cavalier is wise to flee the plague in Italy, for he is searching for a war in which victory is more tangible.

Different from the rest of Defoe's characters is Roxana, who possesses a minimum of courage and comes close to suggesting the stoic ideal of the 'man without passion'. I am not arguing that she has a philosophic calm, but for all her fears and desires she is never carried away by her passions to the extent that she will express her folly in action. At the end of her narrative, when Amy has disappeared with the apparent intention of murdering Susan, Roxana muses on the possibility of confiding in the Quakeress who has shown so much kindness towards her:

. . . it was always a Maxim with me, *that Secrets shou'd never be open'd, without evident Utility*: It cou'd be of no manner of Use to me, or her, to communicate that Part to her; besides, she was too honest herself, to make it safe to me; for tho' she lov'd me very sincerely, and it was plain, by many Circumstances, that she did so, yet she would not Lye for me upon Occasion, as *Amy* wou'd, and therefore it was not advisable on any Terms to communicate that Part. . . .[3]

---

[1] *Journal of the Plague Year*, p. 288.   [2] Ibid., p. 290.
[3] *Fortunate Mistress*, ii. 155.

'Utility' is an important word in Defoe's economic writings. William Walters's warnings to Singleton that fighting without profit was of little utility was typical of Defoe's advice to merchants and tradesmen. He also wrote that 'Usefulness' was '. . . the greatest Pleasure, and justly deem'd by all good Men the truest and noblest End of Life; in which Men come nearest to the Character of our B. Saviour, who went about doing good; and even to that of our great Creator, whose Goodness is over all his Works'.[1] But these ideas should not be confused. There is a vast difference between being useful in good works and a utilitarian morality which evaluates all things according to the profit they bring. Roxana tends to measure every action by a coldly rational standard of self-interest.

Unlike most of Defoe's characters, she almost never forces her actions upon life. She resembles nothing so much as a spider who waits for others to entangle themselves in her web. Whereas Moll wanders through the streets of London to find food or plots to capture a husband, Roxana merely waits until the jeweller, prince, merchant, nobleman, and king come to bestow benefits upon her. Compare her, for example, with Amy, who actively advocates Roxana's surrender to the jeweller, who cries out during the storm at sea in terror and despair and who finally decides that her only means of aiding her mistress is to murder Susan. In all of these circumstances, Roxana merely waits. Sometimes, as in her adventure at sea, she is amazed at her passivity:

I know not what ail'd me, not I; but *Amy* was much more penitent at Sea, and much more sensible of her Deliverance when she Landed, and was safe, than I was; I was in a kind of Stupidity, I know not well what to call it; I had a mind full of Horrour in the time of the Storm, and saw Death before me, as plainly as *Amy*, but my Thoughts got no Vent as *Amy*'s did; I had a silent sullen kind of Grief, which cou'd not break out either in Words or Tears, and which was, therefore, much the worse to bear.[2]

Whatever her inner feelings may be, Roxana preserves an outward calm. She embodies that prudence and *Coldness of the*

[1] *The Case of Protestant Dissenters in Carolina* (1706), p. 9.
[2] *Fortunate Mistress*, i. 148.

Passions' which Pufendorf admired so much. Willa Cather's criticism of her antiseptic qualities is, on the whole, just.[1] Roxana manages to survive, but it is through the attraction which she has for men, not through any kind of courage. Of the heroic virtues, then, Roxana has only application and some capacity, but Defoe reminded his readers that the Devil was pre-eminent in these qualities as well. It is no accident that this 'Queen of Whores' is Defoe's least attractive character.

IV

The Nation's Genius acted from below
Receives no Service, will no Merit know.
Fame's empty Record none but *Marlbro*' shows,
Would *England's* Work on *England's* Terms espouse;
But he, like *William, Heavens their Fame regard,*
Pursues true Vertue for its own Reward.
Welcome Immortal Hero's to that Shore,
Where Men of *equal Worth* were never seen before.
                              DEFOE, *The Double Welcome*[2]

THAT William and Marlborough should make virtue 'its own Reward' seemed miraculous to Defoe, and it is not surprising that Marlborough was later dropped from such a saintly position. Since all men act from self-love, the amazing quality of the hero is that he can postpone his expectation of reward:

The Good Man's Expectation then *must* be
From Happiness with *Immortality*:
Something which to sublimer Vertue's due,
Something substantial and eternal too,
That can for all his Suffering satisfie,
His Hopes support, and all his Wants supply:
For if to future State we've no regard,
How then can Vertue be its own Reward?[3]

---

[1] See 'Defoe's *The Fortunate Mistress*', *On Writing* (1953), pp. 83–85.
[2] In *A True Collection*, ii. 172.
[3] 'The Character of the Late Dr. Samuel Annesley', in *A True Collection*, i. 116.

The true hero, then, must govern his life as if his reward will be heavenly not earthly fame. This alone will enable him to sacrifice his self-interest for the public good. Marlborough achieved earthly glory, but not the heavenly fame of Gustavus and William.

In a letter to *Applebee's Journal* on the death of Marlborough, Defoe suggested that 'these Men, we call Heroes' show the folly of their lives at their funerals. It is not sufficient that their careers are immortalized in histories, romances, and ballads or even in the grateful memories of their countrymen. He asks whether this is the real end of heroes:

> Or is their Business rather to add Virtue and Piety to their Glory, which alone will pass with them into Eternity, and make them truly Immortal? What is Glory without Virtue? A great Man without Religion is no more than a great Beast without a Soul. . . .
> . . . If we believe a future State of Life, a Place for the Rewards of good Men, and for the Punishment of the Haters of Virtue, how full of Heroes and famous Men crowd in among the last! How few Crown'd Heads wear the Crowns of immortal Felicity![1]

We must never under-estimate Defoe's religious beliefs. Strictly speaking, only the Christian hero meets Defoe's standards, only Gustavus and William among all those he admired.

But Defoe seldom strikes such a high moral note. In his novels it is natural law which rules, and the standard for the hero is less rigid. Defoe's heroes and heroines are human, and most are dominated by pride and the accompanying vices of avarice and ambition; yet these are vices which all but the Christian hero will have:

> In the Great Men of the World, take them a degree lower than the Class of Crown'd Heads, he [Satan] has some secret Influence; and hence it comes to pass, that the greatest Heroes, and Men of the highest Character for Atchievements of Glory, either by their Virtue or Valour, however they have been crowned with Victories, and elevated by human Tongues, whatever the most consumate Virtues or good Qualities they have been known by, yet they have always some

Devil or other in them, to preserve *Satan*'s Claim to them uninterrupted, and prevent their Escape out of his Hands; thus we have
seen a bloody Devil in a *D'Alva*; a profligate Devil in a *Buckingham*;
a lying, artful, or politick Devil in a *Richlieu*; a treacherous Devil in a
Mazarin; a cruel, merciless Devil in a *Cortez*; a debauch'd Devil
in an *Eugene*; a conjuring Devil in a *Luxemburg*; and a covetous
Devil in a *M--------h*: In a word, tell me the Man, I tell you
the Spirit that reign'd in him.[1]

In this passage Defoe was adapting Young's *Universal Passion*
for his own purposes, but long before Young wrote, he selected
Pride, not Young's 'Love of Fame', as the ruling passion. Both
Young and Defoe are indebted to the *Satyr against Mankind* for
their theories, although Rochester thought that man's 'dear-
bought Fame' rose from the central passion of fear, while he
regarded pride as the folly which prevented man from understanding his true condition. 'Nature', wrote La Rochefoucauld,
using a theory of pride very similar to that of Rochester, 'who
so wisely has fitted the Organs of our Body to make us happy,
seems likewise to have bestow'd Pride on us, on purpose, as it
were, to save us the pain of knowing our imperfections.'[2]

Defoe frequently used this type of blinding pride as an
example of man's worst folly, and in 'More Reformation', it
appears as an almost irresistible force:

> For Pride's the Native Regent of the Mind,
> And where it rules it ruins all Mankind;
> He that pretends to storm it, may as well
> Assault the very Counterscarp of Hell;
>
> .   .   .   .   .   .
>
> Whom e're this swelling Vapour does possess,
> It never fails their Reason to suppress;
> To struggle with it is a vain Pretence,
> It masters all the Manners and the Sense;
> But above all things, 'tis distinctly shown,
> In that our least Mistakes we scorn to own:
> Go on in Vice, because we hate to mend,
> And won't acknowledge what we can't defend.[3]

---

[1] *Political History of the Devil*, p. 235.
[2] *Moral Reflections*, p. 8.   [3] In *A True Collection*, ii. 34.

In the Spaniards, whose national sin was pride, it took the form of haughtiness, laziness, and religious bigotry. But the same passion is also at work in Moll, when she tries to excuse herself for her murderous thoughts towards the little girl whose necklace she steals. First she blames the parents for allowing the girl to come home by herself; then she suggests that the child was probably in the care of a neglectful maid who had wandered off with her lover. She repeats several times the disclaimer that since she 'did the Child no harm', and had 'given the Parents a just Reproof for their Negligence', she felt little concern over the incident.[1] Defoe probably never reveals a more profound insight into the human mind, for Moll protests too much. Accompanied by shame, pride prevents her from acknowledging her guilt.

For Defoe, pride is the broad basis for all the other passions and vices:

> In Monarchs and Princes it is call'd Ambition;
> In the richer common People, it is call'd Envy;
> In the Female Sex, it is call'd Emulation;
> In the meaner Sort, it is call'd Malice;
> In the Soldier, it is call'd Rage; some would foolishly
> have it pass for Courage, but 'tis nothing but Pride.
> In the Merchant and Tradesman it is call'd Avarice;
> the Dependents upon which are Knavery and Dishonesty,
> Trick, Cheat, Stock-Jobbing and Bubble.[2]

According to Defoe's system, pride replaces Rochester's fear as the source from which all sin flows. Fear is reduced to the 'Second Sin of Nature', or, as in his description of Satan's sins, to a third place below Hobbes's 'Lust of Rule':

Now do but bring all these Things back to their first Principles, and 'tis all Pride; only, that as Subterranean Water running thro' several Sorts of Earth, is ting'd, and receives both Colour and Taste from the Minerals or Soils thro' which it passes, and operates in its

---

[1] *Moll Flanders*, ii. 8. Defoe is describing the worst pride of all, that which blinds a person to his sins and follies. See *The Commentator*, No. 42 (27 May 1720).
[2] Lee, ii. 481.

farther Uses accordingly; so Pride, branch'd thus out, is denomin-
ated from the Temper and Circumstances of the Person it appears
to act in.[1]

Such a revision of Rochester and Hobbes may seem a futile
quibble, but Defoe was not actually trying to improve upon
a psychology which he found entirely adequate for his purposes.
What he was attempting to achieve by substituting pride for
fear as the 'Regent of the Mind' was a synthesis of his religious
and political theories.

Pride becomes Defoe's secular counterpart for original sin—
the levity and folly which he believed to be part of the nature of
man. His longest, if not his most effective, attack on folly
appears in a section of *Mere Nature Delineated* entitled 'Of the
Usefulness and Necessity of Fools in the Present Age'. The
title is promising, but the results are disappointing. Defoe lacked
the gift for this type of playful irony, and the essay is merely
an undirected attack against all irrational conduct, and, more
specifically, against those who have abandoned religion to live
for pleasure alone. The list of fools promises an analysis of
a 'Self-interested ambitious Fool', but the promise remains
unfulfilled. This 'Satyr' upon the 'Vanity and Pride of a self-
wise World' leaves the reader with a feeling that Defoe lacked
sufficient control of his subject.[2]

This same lack of precision also vitiates the novels to some
extent. Almost all of his characters possess some kind of
courage, and although he is sometimes careful to establish
subtle distinctions between the different kinds, Defoe is far less
precise with the more basic qualities of human nature: pride,
lust for power, vanity, ambition, and avarice. Instead of attempting to make distinctions, he grouped them all under pride. Moll,
for example, speaks of her vanity, her desire to find security
(fear of poverty), and her longing to become a gentlewoman.
These may be translated into pride, fear, and ambition, which,
in combination with self-love, is the same as Rochester's psy-

---

[1] Lee, ii. 481. See also *Jure Divino*, bk. vii, pp. 16, 21, 25.
[2] *Mere Nature*, p. 119.

chology. Here, as in the case of his rendering of emotion, Defoe tended to present motivation based on the idea that all human beings are the same, on the abstraction of the natural man. The narrators, with their feelings of guilt and their occasional lapses into pride and vanity, appear to be far more complex and real than the relatively simple self-characterization they present to the reader.

V

The Knowledge of things, not words, make a schollar.

DEFOE, *The Compleat English Gentleman*[1]

THAT Defoe was the master of realism is one of the duller and more inevitable facts of English literary history, but it is not unfitting to return to this fact at the end of a discussion of Defoe's moral philosophy. He was neither an original nor a profound thinker, and his main excellence as a writer was his sense of the importance of external objects and his willingness to describe an event with detailed accuracy. We may learn the topography of London by studying the streets along which Colonel Jack escaped after stealing a purse, and in the *Journal of the Plague Year* Defoe is not afraid of boring his reader by repeating seemingly unimportant details, reprinting the weekly bills of mortality and telling us the exact date on which the weather turned cold. In his *New Voyage round the World* he begins his narrative by sneering at the inability of sailors to tell a good story, their failure to select from the mass of factual material the pertinent details and events. Yet if this had been Defoe's only talent, we would hardly remember him today.

At the beginning of another narrative, this time a short allegory in the *Review*, Defoe called upon his ability to create a picture which would be vivid enough to cure the 'Perverseness' of the English in politics:

For my part, I can't pretend to the Cure, I'll leave that to the Learned; but I may talk a little to you of the Disease, and draw the

[1] p. 212.

Picture of the Thing for you. Perhaps if we could but artfully enough describe the Ugliness and Deformity of the Thing it self, we might stamp some Aversions in Mens Minds to it—By the Doctrine of Idea's it is allow'd, That to Describe a Thing, Ugly, Horrid and Deform'd, is the best way to get Abhorrence in the Minds of the People—and this was the Method of the great Men in the East, in the Ages of Hieroglyphicks, when Things were more accurately Describ'd by Emblems and Figures than Words; and even our Saviour himself took this Method of Introducing the Knowledge of himself into the World, (*viz.*) By Parables and Similitudes.[1]

For Defoe, then, words were merely the means of picturing the idea, the 'Thing it self', in the mind of his reader. According to Locke's theory, the idea might be made clearer by pictures or descriptions, and if we think of Defoe's belief that language was a means of making things seem concrete and vivid, his adherence to realism, to facts and objects, is not surprising.[2] But what is even more important about the passage from the *Review* is his intention to use this talent for a didactic purpose—to create a fable depicting the evil which Sacheverell's sermon brought upon the nation.

Thus in his fiction Defoe professes a commitment to truth and morality. The fiction or 'Parable' must be justified by its purpose, which is truth. 'Things', he wrote, 'seem to appear more lively to the Understanding, and to make a stronger Impression upon the Mind, when they are insinuated under the Cover of some Symbol or Allegory, especially where the Moral is good, and the Application obvious and easy.'[3] Since history is more true than fiction, it is always to be preferred. Historical truth 'is not to be resisted', whereas the best of parables or allegories might be dismissed by the reader as 'the Chimera of a scribbling Head'.[4] Although Defoe frequently attacked 'Romances', he limited his objections to those works which were intended solely for the diversion of the reader without informing

[1] vii. 25a.
[2] See especially *An Essay concerning Human Understanding*, ed. Alexander Fraser (1959), ii. 161–3 (III. xi. 24–25).
[3] *A Collection of Miscellany Letters*, iv. 210.
[4] *The Danger of Court Differences* (1717), p. 16.

him. He objected particularly to the counterfeit autobiographies and false memoirs which, in spite of being published under 'the Shape or Appearance of Historical Truth', were merely romances in disguise, a form in which 'the Writer is himself the Hero of his own Romance'.[1]

But as Defoe once told Harley, the key to truth is the sincerity of the writer's intent. '. . . a Lye', he wrote, 'Does Not Consist in the Indirect Position of words, but in the Design by False Speaking, to Deciev and Injure my Neighbour. . . .' If you deceive a person for his own good, no one will accuse you of lying. 'This is the Dissimulation I Recomend', he continued, 'which is not Unlike what the Apostle Sayes of himself; becoming all Things to all Men, that he might Gain Some. This Hypocrise is a Vertue. . . .'[2] Defoe's argument is sophistic and can hardly be used to justify those parts of his fiction from which no moral whatsoever can be drawn, but it establishes a basis for any type of fiction which contains serious ideas, social commentary, or even a tag moral at the end. It is not surprising therefore to find a defence of moral romance in the middle of his longest attack on the romances of his day:

But on the contrary, where the Moral of the Tale is duly annex'd, and the End directed right, wherein it evidently accords; the enforcing sound Truths; making just and solid Impressions on the Mind; recommending great and good Actions, raising Sentiments of Virtue in the Soul, and filling the Mind with just Resentment against wicked Actions of all Kinds: . . . in such Cases, Fables, feigned Histories, invented Tales, and even such as we call *Romances*, have been allowed as the most pungent Way of writing or speaking; the most apt to make Impressions upon the Mind, and open the Door to the just Inferences and Improvement which was to be made of them.[3]

Although Defoe did not adhere to his own demand that a serious work of fiction should make no pretence at being a genuine autobiography, most of his novels may be regarded as a series of moral fables presented in a vivid and realistic manner.

---

[1] *New Family Instructor*, p. 53.　　　[2] *Letters*, p. 42.
[3] *New Family Instructor*, p. 52.

In treating material from natural law and adapting a psychology for the natural man, Defoe was often treating problems which were extraordinarily abstract, and frequently there is a gap between the realistic technique and the insubstantial theory. In his study of Colonel Jack's marital career, for example, Defoe merely presented the plot outline of a series of marital situations which might have been taken directly from legal texts. There is little attempt to develop character or to investigate the feelings of either his protagonist or his many wives. Instead there is the simple self-love psychology to sketch in human reactions in a kind of shorthand. When this occurs, we seem to see the out-lines of a story in which the moral may be clear but the events and characters are shadowy.

In the preface to the fourth edition of *Colonel Jack* the editor revised Defoe's suggestion that the book might be 'equally useful, and capable of doing good' whether it was 'a History or a Parable' to read: '*Nor is it of any Concern to the Reader, whether it be an exact historical Relation of real Facts, or whether the Hero of it intended to present us, at least in part, with a moral Romance.*' Defoe would probably have felt the expansion of his term 'History' was redundant and that it was going too far to say that the truth of the narration was of no importance, but certainly we can agree that the term 'moral romance' is an improvement over Defoe's clumsy use of 'parable' or his somewhat defensive argument in the *Serious Reflections* that he was '. . . writing a parable or an allusive allegoric history. . . .' *The Fortunate Mistress*, for example, is surely no allegory, but if Defoe began his novel with the intention of writing a secret memoir in the manner of Mrs. Manley, he soon became so involved with Roxana's unnatural attitude towards sex and marriage that he could not resist changing the time sequence of his fable by placing her in the luxurious and unnatural court of Charles II. It may be said, then, that Defoe's insistence on drawing a moral from natural law, if it adds depth and seriousness to his fiction, detracts both from his realistic creation of character and the 'formal realism' of his presentation of events.

But Defoe was not always unsuccessful. Although Moll Flanders may seem more in character when she is quoting Rochester than when she is sermonizing on 'natural' behaviour, her obedience to the law of nature is so implicit that these remarks never seem entirely incongruous. And *Robinson Crusoe* is his most successful work because the hero lives in an environment in which natural law operates without complexity. We have no difficulty translating Crusoe's terrible sense of isolation, his pleasure in the beauty of his island, and his desire for comfort into modern terms.

From this it might be argued that Defoe's use of natural law is entirely satisfactory only when he ignores technical legal questions and concentrates on the broader problems of man's relation to his natural environment. But the problem is not so simple, for without a knowledge of natural law, we cannot understand the morality of Defoe's 'moral romances'. Lacking this key, most critics have examined only Defoe's realistic technique. As a result, if Defoe has been praised for his realism and his ability to tell a good story, he has been condemned for shallow content and a paucity of moral perception. I have tried to show that this judgement is mistaken. When Defoe fails, it is because he has neglected to blend his ideas with his technique, to clarify his moral or to develop his characters sufficiently, not because he was merely a clever journalist trying to provide light entertainment.

LIST OF BOOKS MENTIONED

A. DEFOE

The Anatomy of Exchange-Alley. London, 1719.
An Apology for the Army. London, 1715.
An Argument Proving that the Design of Employing and Enobling Foreigners, Is a Treasonable Conspiracy against the Constitution. London, 1717.
Atalantis Major. Edinburgh, 1711.
The Candidate. London, 1715.
The Case of Protestant Dissenters in Carolina. London, 1706.
Chickens Feed Capons. London, 1731 [1730].
A Collection of Miscellany Letters Selected out of Mist's Weekly Journal. 4 vols. London, 1722–7.
The Commentator. London, 1720.
The Compleat English Gentleman, ed. Karl D. Bülbring. London, 1890.
The Compleat English Tradesman. 2 vols. London, 1727.
The Conduct of Christians Made the Sport of Infidels. London, 1717.
The Conduct of Robert Walpole. London, 1717.
The Danger of Court Differences. London, 1717.
The Earlier Life and Chief Earlier Works of Daniel Defoe, ed. Henry Morley. London, 1889, for the following:
  The Consolidator.
  An Essay upon Projects.
An Enquiry into the Case of Mr. Asgil's General Translation. London, 1704.
An Essay upon Buying and Selling of Speeches. London, 1716.
The Evident Approach of a War and Something of the Necessity of It. London, 1727.
The Four Years Voyages of Capt. George Roberts. London, 1726.
A General History of the Robberies and Murders of the Most Notorious Pyrates. 2 vols. London, 1724–8.
A General History of Trade. London, 1713.
A General Pardon Consider'd. London, 1717.
Good Advice to the Ladies. London, 1702.
The Great Law of Subordination Consider'd. London, 1724.
An Historical Account of the Voyages and Adventures of Sir Walter Raleigh. London, 1719 [1720].
The History of the Wars of his Present Majesty, Charles XII. London, 1720.

A Hymn to the Mob. London, 1715.
The Interest of the Several Princes and States of Europe Consider'd.
    London, 1698.
Jure Divino. London, 1706.
The Letters of Daniel Defoe, ed. George Healey. Oxford, 1955.
Madagascar: or, Robert Drury's Journal. London, 1729.
Memoirs of Captain Carleton, ed. Cyril Hartman. London, 1929.
Memoirs of the Conduct of Her Late Majesty and Her Last Ministry.
    London, 1715.
Mercurius Politicus. London, 1716–20.
Mere Nature Delineated. London, 1726.
A New Family Instructor. London, 1727.
The Novels and Miscellaneous Works of Daniel De Foe. 20 vols. Oxford,
    1841, for the following:
    The Family Instructor.
    An Humble Proposal to the People of England.
    Religious Courtship.
*The Original Power of the Collective Body of the People of England,
    Examined and Asserted.* London, 1702 [1701].
Party-Tyrrany, in Narratives of Early Carolina 1650–1708, ed. Alex-
    ander Salley. New York, 1911.
The Political History of the Devil. London, 1726.
The Protestant Jesuite Unmask'd. London, 1704.
*Reasons Humbly Offer'd for a Law to Enact the Castration of Popish
    Ecclesiastics.* London, 1700.
Reflections upon the Late Great Revolution. London, 1689.
Remarks on the Bill to Prevent Frauds Committed by Bankrupts.
    London, 1706.
A Review of the Affairs of France, ed. Arthur W. Secord (Facsimile
    Text Society. Publication no. 44). 22 vols. New York, 1938.
Rogues on Both Sides. London, 1711.
Romances and Narratives by Daniel Defoe, ed. George Aitken. 16 vols.
    London, 1895, for the following:
    Adventures of Captain John Gow.
    Colonel Jacque.
    Due Preparations for the Plague.
    The Dumb Philosopher.
    A Narrative of All the Robberies of John Sheppard.
    A Narrative of the Proceedings in France.
    Serious Reflections of Robinson Crusoe.
*The Shakespeare Head Edition of the Novels and Selected Writings of
    Daniel Defoe.* 14 vols. Oxford, 1927, for the following:
    An Appeal to Honour and Justice.
    Captain Singleton.
    Colonel Jack.
    The Fortunate Mistress.
    A Journal of the Plague Year.

Memoirs of a Cavalier.

Moll Flanders.

A Plan of the English Commerce.

The Poor Man's Plea.

Robinson Crusoe (with *The Farther Adventures of Robinson Crusoe*).

A True and Genuine Account of the Life and Actions of the Late Jonathan Wild.

The True Born Englishman.

A Short Narrative of the Life and Actions of His Grace John D. of Marlborough. London, 1711.

Some Considerations upon Street-Walkers. London, 1726.

A Speech without Doors. London, 1710.

Street-Robberies, Consider'd. London, 1728.

A True Collection of the Writings of the Author of the True-Born Englishman. 2 vols. London, 1703–5, for the following:

The Character of the Late Dr. Samuel Annesly by Way of Elegy.

The Danger of the Protestant Religion.

The Double Welcome.

The Mock Mourners.

More Reformation.

The Unreasonableness and Ill Consequences of Imprisoning the Body for Debt. London, 1729.

The Wickedness of a Disregard to Oaths. London, 1723.

B. SECONDARY SOURCES

ABU BAKR IBN AL-TUFAIL. *The Improvement of Human Reason*, trans. Simon Ockley. London, 1708.

JOSEPH ADDISON, RICHARD STEELE, *et al.* *The Spectator*, ed. George Gregory Smith. Everyman Library ed. 4 vols. London, 1911.

CORNELIUS AGRIPPA. *The Vanity of Arts and Sciences.* London, 1676.

A. OWEN ALDRIDGE. 'Polygamy and Deism', *JEGP*, xlviii (July 1949), 343–60.

WILLIAM AMES. *Conscience.* London, 1643.

THOMAS AQUINAS. *Summa Theologica*, trans. Fathers of the English Dominican Province. 21 vols. London, 1922.

ARISTOTLE. *Politics*, in *Works*, trans. Benjamin Jowett. 12 vols. Oxford, 1908–52.

MARY ASTELL. *A Serious Proposal to the Ladies.* London, 1697.

ARTHUR BARKER. *Milton and the Puritan Dilemma.* Toronto, 1942.

RICHARD BAXTER. *Practical Works.* 4 vols. London, 1707.

PIERRE BAYLE. *The Dictionary*, trans. Pierre Desmaizeaux. 5 vols. London, 1734.

APHRA BEHN. *The Royal Slave*, in *The Novels of Mrs. Aphra Behn*, ed. Ernest Baker. London, 1913.

RICHARD BLACKMORE. *The Nature of Man.* London, 1717.

JAMES BURNET, Lord Monboddo. *Of the Origin and Progress of Language.* 2nd ed. 6 vols. Edinburgh, 1774.

THOMAS BURNET. *The Sacred Theory of the Earth.* 3rd ed. London, 1697.

JOHN BUTLER. *The True Case of John Butler.* London, 1697.

JOSEPH BUTLER. *Works,* ed. William Gladstone. 2 vols. Oxford, 1896.

JOHN CALVIN. *Institutes of the Christian Religion,* trans. Henry Beveridge. 2 vols. London, 1953.

ROBERT CARLYLE and A. J. CARLYLE. *A History of Medieval Political Theories in the West.* 6 vols. Edinburgh, 1950.

WILLA CATHER. *On Writing.* New York, 1953.

PIERRE CHARRON. *Of Wisdom,* trans. George Stanhope. 3 vols. London, 1707.

MARCUS TULLIUS CICERO. *De Inventione,* trans. H. M. Hubbel. Loeb Library ed. London, 1949.

JOHN CLARKE. *An Enquiry into the Cause and Origin of Moral Evil.* 2 vols. London, 1720–1.

JOHN CLARKE. *An Examination of the Notion of Moral Goodness and Evil.* London, 1725.

SAMUEL TAYLOR COLERIDGE. *Miscellaneous Criticism,* ed. Thomas Raysor. Cambridge, Mass., 1936.

Concubinage and Polygamy Disprov'd. London, 1698.

EDWARD COOKE. *A Voyage to the South Sea.* 2 vols. London, 1712.

ANTHONY COOPER, Lord Shaftesbury. *Characteristics,* ed. John Robertson. 2 vols. London, 1900.

GATIEN DE COURTILZ, sieur de Sandras. *Mémoires de Mr. L. C. D. R.* Paris, 1691.

MAURICE CRANSTON. *John Locke.* London, 1957.

RICHARD CUMBERLAND. *A Treatise of the Laws of Nature,* trans. John Maxwell. London, 1728.

RENÉ DESCARTES. *Philosophical Works,* trans. Elizabeth Haldane and G. R. T. Ross. 2 vols. New York, 1955.

JOHN EACHARD. *Mr. Hobb's State of Nature Considered.* London, 1672.

JACQUES ÉSPRIT. *Discourses on the Deceitfulness of Humane Virtues,* trans. William Beauvoir. London, 1706.

GABRIEL DE FOIGNY. *A New Discovery of Terra Incognita Australis,* trans. John Dunton. London, 1693.

BERNARD DE FONTENELLE. *A Plurality of Worlds,* trans. John Glanvill. London, 1929.

GARCILASO DE LA VEGA. *Royal Commentaries of the Yncas,* trans. Clements Markham. 2 vols. London, 1869.

OTTO GIERKE. *Natural Law and the Theory of Society,* trans. Ernest Barker. Cambridge, England, 1950.

JEAN GIRAUDOUX. *Suzanne and the Pacific,* trans. Ben Redman. New York, 1923.

LEW GIRDLER. 'Defoe's Education at Newington Green', *SP,* 1 (October 1953), 573–91.

KATHLEEN GRANGE. *Doctor Johnson and the Passions*. Unpublished Dissertation. University of California at Los Angeles, 1960.
HUGO GROTIUS. *De Jure Belli ac Pacis*, trans. Francis Kelsey. 2 vols. Oxford, 1925.
RICHARD HAKLUYT. *The Principal Navigations of the English Nation*. 12 vols. Glasgow, 1903–5.
WALTER HAMMOND. *A Paradox*, in *Harleian Miscellany*. 12 vols. London, 1808–11, xi. 534–43.
MATTHEW HENRY. *An Exposition of the New and Old Testament*. 4th ed. London, 1737.
Historical Manuscripts Commission. 8th report. London, 1907.
The History of the Bermudaes, ed. J. Henry Lefroy. London, 1882.
THOMAS HOBBES. *The Elements of Law*, ed. Ferdinand Tönnies. Cambridge, England, 1928.
—— *Leviathan*, ed. A. R. Waller. Cambridge, England, 1935.
—— *Tripos*. 3rd ed. London, 1684.
RICHARD HOOKER. *Laws of Ecclesiastical Polity*. Everyman Library ed. 4 vols. London, 1954.
DAVID HUME. *Treatise of Human Nature*, ed. L. A. Selby-Bigge. Oxford, 1888.
FRANCIS HUTCHESON. *An Inquiry concerning the Original of Our Ideas of Virtue or Moral Good*, in *British Moralists*, ed. L. A. Selby-Bigge. 2 vols. Oxford, 1897, i. 70–177.
It Cannot Rain but It Pours. London, 1726.
ISAAC JAMES. *Providence Displayed*. Bristol, 1800.
FLAVIUS JOSEPHUS. *The Jewish War*, in *Works*, trans. H. St. J Thackeray and Ralph Marcus. Loeb Library ed. 9 vols. London, 1926– .
CHARLES KINGSLEY. 'Introduction', in Defoe, *The Surprising Adventures of Robinson Crusoe*. London, 1868.
LOUIS KRONENBERGER. *Kings and Desperate Men*. New York, 1959.
LUCIUS LACTANTIUS. *Works*, trans. William Fletcher. (*Ante-Nicene Christian Library*, vols. xxi–xxii). Edinburgh, 1871.
FRANÇOIS, DUC DE LA ROCHEFOUCAULD. *Moral Reflections and Maxims*. London, 1706.
WILLIAM LEE. *Daniel Defoe: His Life and Recently Discovered Writings*. 3 vols. London, 1869.
ANTOINE LE GRANDE. *Man without Passion*, trans. G. R. London, 1675.
ROGER L'ESTRANGE. *The Fables of Aesop*. 2 vols. London, 1704.
Librorum ex Bibliothecis Philippi Farewell, D.D. et Danielis Defoe. London, 1731.
JOHN LOCKE. *An Essay concerning Human Understanding*, ed. Alexander Frazer. 2 vols. New York, 1959.
—— *Essays on the Law of Nature*, ed. W. von Leyden. Oxford, 1954.
—— *Some Thoughts concerning Education*, in *On Politics and Education*, ed. Howard Penniman. New York, 1947.

JOHN LOCKE. *Two Treatises of Civil Government.* Everyman Library ed. London, 1954.

ARTHUR LOVEJOY. *Essays in the History of Ideas.* Baltimore, 1948.

JAMES LOWDE. *A Discourse concerning the Nature of Man.* London, 1694.

NICCOLÒ MACHIAVELLI. *The Discourses,* trans. Leslie Walker. 2 vols. London, 1950.

BERNARD MANDEVILLE. *The Fable of the Bees,* ed. F. B. Kaye. 2 vols. Oxford, 1957.

The Manifesto of Lord Peter. London, 1726.

Memoirs for the Curious. No. 1. London, 1701.

Miscellaneous Poems, ed. David Lewis. London, 1726.

MICHEL DE MONTAIGNE. *The Essays,* trans. E. J. Trechmann. New York, 1950.

CHARLES DE SECONDAT, Baron de Montesquieu. *Persian Letters,* trans. John Davidson. London, 1902.

—— *The Spirit of the Laws,* trans. Thomas Nugent. New York, 1949.

JOHN ROBERT MOORE. 'The Canon of Defoe's Writings', *The Library,* xi (September 1956), 155–69.

—— *Daniel Defoe.* Chicago, 1958.

—— '*The Tempest* and *Robinson Crusoe*', *RES,* xxi (January 1945), 52–56.

HENRY NEVILLE. *The Isle of Pines,* in *Shorter Novels,* ed. Philip Henderson. 3 vols. Everyman Library ed. London, 1929–30, ii. 225–35.

—— *A New and Further Discovery of the Isle of Pines.* London, 1668.

JOHN NORRIS. *A Collection of Miscellanies,* 3rd ed. London, 1699.

MAXIMILLIAN NOVAK. *Economics and the Fiction of Daniel Defoe* (University of California Studies in English). Berkeley, 1962.

JOHN OLDMIXON. *The British Empire in America.* 2 vols. London, 1741.

SAMUEL PARKER. *A Demonstration of the Divine Authority of the Law of Nature and of the Christian Religion.* London, 1681.

A. C. R. PASTOR. *The Idea of Robinson Crusoe.* Watford, 1930.

ROY HARVEY PEARCE. *The Savages of America.* Baltimore, 1953.

SPIRO PETERSON. 'The Matrimonial Theme of Defoe's Roxana', *PMLA,* lxx (March 1955), 166–91.

ALEXANDER POPE. *Correspondence,* ed. George Sherburn. 5 vols. Oxford, 1956.

'Préface', *La Vie et les Avantures de Robinson Crusoe.* Amsterdam, 1720.

SAMUEL PUFENDORF. *De Officio Hominis et Civis,* trans. Frank More. 2 vols. Oxford, 1927.

—— *An Introduction to the History of Europe,* trans. Joseph Sayer. 2 vols. London, 1769.

SAMUEL PUFENDORF. *Of the Law of Nature and Nations*, trans. Basil Kennett. Oxford, 1703.

SAMUEL PURCHAS. *Hackluytus Posthumus*. 20 vols. Glasgow, 1905–1907.

WOODES ROGERS. *A Cruising Voyage round the World*, in *Romances and Narratives by Daniel Defoe*, ed. George Aitken. 16 vols. London, 1895, iii. 317–24.

JEAN-JACQUES ROUSSEAU. *Emile*, trans. Barbara Foxley. Everyman Library ed. London, 1911.

—— *The Social Contract and Discourses*, trans. G. D. H. Cole. Everyman Library ed. London, 1955.

HENRY SACHEVERELL. *The New Association*, part II. London, 1703.

THOMAS SALMON. *A Critical Essay concerning Marriage*. London, 1724.

ARTHUR W. SECORD. *Studies in the Narrative Method of Daniel Defoe* (University of Illinois Studies in Language and Literature, vol. ix, no. 1). Urbana, 1924.

JOHN FRANCIS SENAULT. *The Use of the Passions*, trans. Henry Cary. London, 1671.

J. SHAFTE. *The Great Law of Nature or Self-Preservation, Examined, Asserted, and Vindicated from Mr. Hobbes His Abuses*. London, 1673.

ALGERNON SIDNEY. *Discourses concerning Government*. 3rd ed. London, 1751.

A. L. SINGH and ROBERT ZINGG. *Wolf Children and Feral Man*. New York, 1942.

ADAM SMITH. *The Wealth of Nations*. Everyman Library ed. 2 vols. London, 1954.

JOHN SMITH. *Works*, ed. Edward Arber. Birmingham, 1884.

BENEDICT SPINOZA. *A Treatise Partly Theological and Partly Political*. London, 1689.

RUDOLF STAMM. *Der Aufgeklärte Puritanismus Daniel Defoes* (Swiss Studies in English, vol. i). Zürich, 1936.

RICHARD STEELE. *The Englishman*, December 1–3, 1713, in *Romances and Narratives by Daniel Defoe*, ed. George Aitken. 16 vols. London, 1895, iii. 324–8.

LEO STRAUSS. *Natural Right and History*. Chicago, 1953.

JAMES SUTHERLAND. *Defoe*. London, 1950.

JONATHAN SWIFT. *Prose Works*, ed. Herbert Davis. 13 vols. Oxford, 1939– .

—— *Poems*, ed. Harold Williams. 3 vols. Oxford, 1958.

WILLIAM TEMPLE. 'An Essay upon the Original and Nature of Government', in *Miscellanea*. 5th ed. London, 1697.

ERNEST TUVESON. 'The Origin of the Moral Sense', *HLQ*, xi (May 1948), 242–59.

JAMES TYRRELL. *A Brief Disquisition of the Law of Nature*. London, 1693.

DENIS VAIRASSE. *The History of the Sevarites.* London, 1675.

LUDWIG VISCHER, trans. *Das Leben und die ganze ungemeine Bege-
benheiten des Robinson Crusoe.* 6th ed. Leipzig, 1721.

HOWARD WARRENDER. *The Political Philosophy of Hobbes.* Oxford,
1957.

IAN WATT. *The Rise of the Novel.* London, 1957.

JOHN WILMOT, EARL OF ROCHESTER. *Poems,* ed. Vivian de Sola Pinto.
London, 1953.

WALTER WILSON. *Memoirs of the Life and Times of Daniel De Foe.*
3 vols. London, 1830.

EDWARD YOUNG. *Works.* 3 vols. London, 1802.

JOHANN ZIMMERMANN. *Solitude.* 2 vols. London, 1800.

INDEX